PERSONAL DEVELOPMENT

THE KEY TO SUCCESS

Dr. Drissa Kone

To my Mother Yah,

who taught me about real love by her sacrifice

Table of Contents

Preface

As you open this book, you are certainly curious about what "personal development" means. I would like to spare you from dictionary definitions for now and begin by telling you a story. I once asked one of my students this question, "When you finish your studies, what are you going to do?" He replied with confidence, "When I finish my studies, I will have a high paying job, in one of the best companies. And I am going to marry a beautiful and intelligent woman. We will have beautiful children. We will grow old happily together and retire in California." I smiled and said to myself, "What a beautiful but naive way of perceiving life!"

Unfortunately, a successful life has never been that simple to achieve. Unexpected challenges will come your way and if you are not internally prepared, it will be a total disaster. You can end up carrying resentments and revenge until you die. So, I asked my student a few follow up questions: "What if you end up being wrongly arrested and jailed like Mandela? How will you handle such a situation? What if one day you go to the doctor and he tells you that you have cancer? What are you going to do? How about if one of your children is born with a disability or even becomes a drug addict? What are you going to do if you are paralyzed after a car accident?"

I am sure you might also be thinking what you will do when you face these kinds of challenges, right? Life come as a package with many surprises and challenges and sometimes with unbearable experiences. Personal development allows you to tap into your inner potential and face the challenges of the moment and transform your life in a meaningful way. It is the key for a successful life. This includes both your personal and professional life.

Usually, we face five major roadblocks on the path to success. Franciscan ethicist Richard Rohr, in his book titled *Adam's Return*, explains how to transform these five steps to our advantage. First, we must accept that life is hard; nothing is easy. So, no need to run away from pain; it is part of the deal. Drugs and other pain killers will only help momentarily, and then you will face the reality of life again. Turn your pain into a sacred gift and give this gift to the world. Every time you face a challenge, look at the other side of the coin. You will see meaning in your pain and that is how the process of healing begins. You will not only heal yourself but those who can identify with you. If you play the victim or blame game, if you complain, you will repeat the failures of history and transmit your pain to the next generation. If you do not transform your pain, you will transmit it to the next generation.

Second, you are not the center of the universe, the Creator of the universe is. Therefore, you don't need to worry too much about your image; ultimately you don't always have to be right.

2

Often, it is better to have peace than to be right at all costs. When you put yourself first, you will end worshiping yourself. This is called self-idolatry or being a megalomaniac. So be careful about superiority complexes based on religion, race, social position, or age. The truth is that we are all fundamentally equal before the Creator of the universe. As the scripture says, love your neighbor as yourself.

Third, your life does not belong to you. It also belongs to your family, to your community, to your nation and to the world. So, do not be selfish; think of others. Don't make decisions that are good only for you. Think about how they impact others. No relationship will last long when both partners think about themselves first. Selfishness will lead to self-destruction and regret.

Fourth, you are not 100% in control of your life. Everything that happens to you happens for a reason, and you don't need to know the answer to everything. If you do your best to get something and it doesn't happen, there is a reason why it did not happen. Therefore, there is no need to worry too much as you can try again. If you apply for a job and do not get hired, no need to make a big deal out it. Keep moving forward with your life. If you are fired from your job for whatever reason, move forward and rebuild yourself. Nothing happens by chance; a failure today leads to a success tomorrow. If people say no to you today it can be a tremendous blessing, but you may only realize later it was a blessing.

Lastly, you are going to die someday. We all going to take that last breath, so it is better to gradually let go of the things we are too attached to. Either way, we can't take to the grave those things we are attached to in the physical world. Let go of material possessions; it is a biggest illusion ever. We are not the owners of material things, we are stewards. We use them for a period of time and then we pass them on to the next generation. Do not miss the point of life running after material things and forget about your relationships. As the Dalai Lama said once, "Human beings live like they will never die, and they end up dying like they never lived." Life is short, so live a meaningful life.

There are many philosophical views on personal development. What is presented here is based on Carl Jung's school of thought. Carl Gustav Jung (July 26, 1875 – June 6, 1961) was a Swiss psychiatrist and psychoanalyst, and the founder of analytical psychology. One of his most important quotes is: "Until you make the unconscious conscious, it will direct your life and you will call it fate." Many people believe that their life is the product of random causes and that, in most cases, they cannot do much about it.

Anytime you engage in an activity, do you think first about the result or the process? Is the result exciting enough for you to the point that you will overcome all the challenges in the process? Are you passionate enough about the result, the outcome, the goal or even your dream to the point that you will not easily give up when challenges arise? Most people think about the result, and when they encounter difficulties in the process they naturally give up.

In fact, the question should be asked first, "what does it take to complete this task," and then, "what will be the result." As George A. Sheehan put it "Success means having the courage, the determination, and the will to become the person you believe you were meant to be." The amount of courage and determination you invest in the process determines your success. For example, if you want to learn about personal development and you pick up this book, the process will be to entirely read the book and the result will be the knowledge gained. Do you want to become an expert in personal development? You must gain knowledge about personal development, and you pay the price of mastering the skills needed to guide others. You would like to coach others; you must pay the price to train yourself and reach the level of mastery. The process is the effort, consistency, determination and courage to get the result. More importantly, stumbling and falling is part of the process and not considered failure. If you feel tired, take a rest and then keep going. That is part of the process and the learning experience. The real meaning of failure is when you give up on the process.

Our thoughts, feelings, judgments and actions are driven by our unconscious mind, as Carl Jung said. The unconscious mind is where memories, dreams and unmet expectations are stored. Therefore, when we engage in an activity, even though the result may be something we dream of, when challenges come our decisions are impacted by our unconscious mind. This is also referred to as the "shadow," which become the invisible driver of our moment-to-moment decision making. Nothing great can be accomplished without constant investment over time. Once again, Carl Jung pointed out: "It is not by looking at the light that one becomes luminous, but by plunging into its darkness. But this work is often unpleasant, therefore unpopular."

It is essential to revisit our own shadow materials, which have built up from our childhood through our adult life, to understand how we are being impacted. Shadow materials are usually issues that have not been properly processed and are hidden in the subconscious or unconscious level. These issues are triggered by current life challenges and people we are in relationship with. Being unaware of our own shadow will eventually prevent us from properly addressing life challenges we face, and lead us to wrong choices and regrets.

Most people blame others whenever something goes wrong in their life, and never look at themselves in the mirror. The most rewarding exercise for every individual who is genuinely seeking self-improvement, personal growth and development is to engage in what Ken Wilber refers to as "shadow boxing." Whenever we are angry, sad or frustrated, instead of blaming someone we exercise self-reflection, self-criticism and self-control. Anger, frustration and disappointment towards life and others are related to our own unresolved issues; they are never 100% about others.

For example, if someone misbehaves in your workplace and you feel constantly angry toward that person, you can come up with all kinds of arguments to explain why that person is not doing the right thing. These are only partially true, because the reason why it is bothering you that much is that you have internal issues that you have not properly processed. Even if you leave your workplace for another one, you will certainly encounter the same emotional difficulties with another person. It is similar in relationships. People who break up or divorce thinking it is all their partner's fault will face the same difficulties in their next relationship. Until they learn the lesson, the same pattern will keep repeating itself.

The shadow self has to be addressed from within, and unless it is done, you will not move to the next stage of your life. You can develop good communication techniques to address the issue of anger with others, but if you cannot handle your internal state of being while you are challenged, all these techniques will fall apart at a certain point. A wisdom tradition puts it well: Every time you stumble and fall, look around, there is a beautiful diamond that certainly caused the fall. Most people, instead of looking for the diamond, want to know who pushed them to the ground and how they can make someone pay for it. Stumbling and falling can be rewarding when we have a positive attitude.

Life is like the two sides of the same coin. Do not get stuck on looking at only one side of the coin, because the other side also has a message for you. Receiving that message might transform your life for the better. The process can sometimes be very painful. However, you must understand that life and pain are inseparable; there is no life without pain. In other words, no pain no gain. No one can avoid pain and suffering, but pain and growth are two sides of the same coin. The way you react to your pain will determine your growth and success. Your reaction to pain is what leads you to growth and happiness or regret and unhappiness. This is one of the most fundamental teachings in personal development. It is the key to unlock your potential.

PART I: Personal Development Theories

Chapter 1: Born for a reason

Personal story

I was born and raised in a small village in the northern part of Ivory Coast in West Africa. The day was I was born, there was heavy rain in my village. My father perceived my birth as a divine message to the family. He was very happy that I was a boy and he decided to consult a seer to predict my future. The seer told him that I would be an Imam (spiritual guide in the Islamic community) in the future. My father decided to name me Drissa. Drissa, or Idris, in Arabic means instructor or teacher or guide. Idris is a highly respected prophet in the Islamic tradition, the same figure as Enoch in the Bible. He was given the name "Idris" which comes from the Arabic word "dirasah" which means "lengthy study." He is called Idris because he studied deeply what was revealed to Prophet Adam and Prophet Seth. Prophet Enoch/Idris called the people of his time to a genuine religious life. He called the people to live a non-luxurious life, as Prophet Muhammad did in his time. Among his famous words of wisdom were, "Being patient, while believing in God, leads one to victory." This was engraved on the stone in his ring.

My passion for education might have something to do with my name Idris or Drissa. When I was 5 years old, I wanted to go to school even though the age to enter elementary school was 7 or 8 years. I cried so much that my father decided to break the rule so I could go to school earlier than usual. I was not a brilliant student, but I just loved being in school. The learning environment was fascinating, and I loved the smell of my school bag and the new books. I loved readings stories. I also enjoy explaining to other what I had learned in books.

When I was in 6th grade, I worked hard to pass the final exam to go to middle school, but I could not pass. I was feeling devasted and decided not to go back to school anymore. My teacher visited me and convinced me that it was worth trying again. He also convinced my parents to give me another chance. While talking to me he said something that remains in my mind forever. He had my gradebook with him, and on the cover, you could see a man teaching another person. He said, "Look at this man in the picture. When you grow up you will become a great teacher like him." My vision to become a teacher was born through this experience with my elementary teacher. It is was a life changing moment. It seems like something was planted in me. I believe my passion for teaching was born out of that experience.

Eventually, I went back to school and did very well in all my exams. I even exceeded all expectations. In middle school and high school, I did very well. I became fascinated with books in the fields of philosophy, history and biographies. I was also drawn into any topic related to spirituality and mysticism. I can still remember books that made a lasting impact on me. Some of them are *L'Etranger* by Albert Camus, *L'Aventure Ambiguë* by Cheikh Hamidou Kane, *Cahier d'un Retour au Pays Natal* by Aime Cesaire, *Peau Noir Masques Blancs* by Frantz Fanon, *Les Frasques d'Ebinto* by Amadou Kone, *Les Soleils des Independences* by Ahmadou Kourouma, and many other books that I think expanded my consciousness.

After obtaining my high school diploma in 1999, I successfully passed the teacher examination that year and went through two years training to become a K-12 school teacher. Ten years after the vision I had when I was in elementary school, my dream became a reality. However, another journey had also begun.

In 2003, I was invited to attend a seminar on spirituality. I went to the seminar because I was just recovering from a tragedy in my life. I was unjustly arrested and tortured, mistakenly accused of being a rebel during the civil war in the country. I was wondering and asking myself why do bad things happen to good people. Why I must go through such suffering when I did not do anything wrong? What was the purpose of this absurdity? Why did God, the almighty, allow this to happen to me? These questions influenced me to attend a religious seminar, expecting to get answers to my existential questions.

I was happily surprised to learn that there are universal principles in life and when you know these principles and practice them constantly you will be successful in whatever you are doing. At the end of the seminar, I said to myself, I would like to teach these principles to university students in the future. I then started to study in depth the book called *Divine Principle* written by Rev. Sun Myung Moon. I also taught the *Divine Principle* content several times.

Later I came to realize that it would be difficult to reach a larger audience, and more specifically college students, unless it was contextualized. The *Divine Principle* book was purely theological, and its purpose was to convert people to a Unification faith. It was also targeting Christians first.

What stood out for me was the fact that the *Divine Principle* book contained universal principles, and they could transform people's lives without necessarily changing their faith tradition. I took on the challenge to excerpt the universal principles from the *Divine Principle* book. I reorganized the content and adapted it for the audience of university and college students, including young professionals. I also backed up the universal principles with theories in the fields of psychology, sociology and human development. Finally, I developed my own program to train others focusing on personal growth, which eventually leads to success in one's personal and professional life.

As a K-12 teacher, I also pursued a BA in American Studies at the National University of Cocody, now called the Université Félix Houphouët-Boigny, and graduated in 2007. The following year, I left my country and moved to the United States. My passion for education became my priority. From 2010 to 2016, I worked hard to obtain my Masters and my doctoral degrees. As an immigrant from a francophone African country, this was the path for me to integrate into American society. My first Masters was in Theology at the Unification Theological Seminary (UTS) and the second in Diplomacy at Norwich University, a military school in Vermont; and my doctoral degree is in Practical Theology focusing on Peace and Justice at UTS.

The quest for knowledge is a passion for me, but more than ever sharing knowledge became my profession. In 2017, I was hired as a professor of Conflict Resolution at UTS. Since then, I have invested my time and energy in that field of study. I love to see my students getting inspired and empowered to make the world a better place.

My passion for coaching and mentoring in personal development began in 2013 when I came across the book *The 7 Habits of Highly Effective People* by Stephen R. Covey. I have read the book several times. After a few years, the book became part of my everyday life. It was like a sacred book for me. I applied the suggestions in my personal and professional life, and it was such a transformative experience. I also read many other books in the area of success and personal growth, including *Think and Grow Rich* by Napoleon Hill, *The Power of Now* by Eckhart Tolle, *Outwitting the Devil* by Napoleon Hill, *How to Win Friends and Influence People* by Dale Carnegie, *The Four Agreements* by Don Miguel Ruiz, *Radical Forgiveness* by Colin Tipping, and *Developing the Leader Within You* by John C. Maxwell. I highly recommend these books to anyone who is interested in self-improvement.

More importantly, I started to share the ideas of personal development with people around me. I enjoy talking to people about the principles of self-improvement, self-discovery and self-awareness. I could see quite a few people getting inspired when they heard me speak. My first student in this area was my spouse, and it saved my marriage in so many ways. My relationships with my spouse and my kids improved and my professional life became much better than I could imagine. I consider myself an expert the field of personal development today, and in the next ten years I would like to be internationally recognized as a contributor in the field. I will make it my mission to make the personal development program available to college student so that they can improve their personal and professional lives.

Why personal development?

According to Franck Jaotombo, an expert in personal development and work fulfillment, personal development is generally defined as "the conscious pursuit of personal growth by expanding self-awareness and knowledge and improving personal skills." This means that all activities that help develop a knowledge of self, value one's talents and potential, improve one's quality of life, and achieve personal aspirations and dreams are considered personal development. More than self-fulfillment, it is also the desire to continuously improve ourselves by expressing our full potential. Danilo Martuccelli, a professor of sociology at Paris Descartes University in France, considers personal development not to be "psychotherapy but a constant self-improvement" in all areas of life, such as physical, emotional, mental and spiritual.

One essential reason why we need to develop ourselves in this fast-changing postmodern world is for the demands of the workforce. The need for better results and better professionalism is in demand. There is no doubt that constant self-improvement plays a major role in personal and professional success. The ability to overcome the challenges we face in life with a positive mindset is one of the most important criteria for effectiveness. The ability to work and collaborate with others as a team player to achieve a common purpose is one of the most important skills in professional life. By providing training in personal development to students and young professionals, we want to help resolve certain shortcomings that they might not be aware of and to provide some of the essential tools that each person requires for personal and professional development.

Didier Pénissard, a coach in personal development and author of several books in the field, stated that "personal development teaches us how to overcome our internal challenges which sometimes paralyze us." For example, if you are given a position of responsibility in your workplace, or you are asked to reach a goal to complete an important new mission, you will face yourself. Your "fears" and "doubts" might come out as your personal limitations and may stand as obstacles to the achievement of your ambitions. Personal development helps you draw from the subconscious mind to move forward. The human brain has almost unlimited capacity, according to studies in positive psychology, and potential that has never been exploited.

Personal development practices all have a common outcome, knowing yourself and keep improving yourself in order to be successful in your life. Some people practice alone, others in groups. It is up to you to choose the best approach, depending on your present and future needs. I recommend reading books, attending workshops and conferences, but more importantly find a professional coach or a mentor to support you. Personal development is normally for anyone who is seeking self-improvement. However, it is crucial for leaders and managers to absolutely to familiarize themselves with personal development as they constantly deal with daily stress in the workplace. From time to time, couples having difficulties might need personal development to improve their relationship. Additionally, college students need personal development to maximize success in school. I remember teaching a seminar at one of the universities in Ivory Coast in 2016. At the end of the program, most of the students petitioned for the training to be included in their curriculum. I decided to pursue that goal as my next challenge to integrate personal development in the university curriculum in Ivory Coast.

I came to the conclusion that the challenges of our society will not find lasting solutions without making personal development an integral part of our lives. Despite all the political and economic programs that we put in place, without personal development they will sooner or later be doomed to failure. Any education system put in place without personal development will have a high likelihood of failure. In reality, division, hatred, wars and all kind of corruption are due to a lack of personal development.

For example, a religious leader who exploits his members for his own sake using the name of God, is lacking personal development. A business manager who is unable to manage his own emotions is lacking personal development. A political or organizational leader who cannot listen to others is lacking personal development. A professor who thinks he knows best and always argues to be right is, without doubt, lacking personal development. The use of violence to achieve any means is due to a lack of personal development. Egocentric, ethnocentric behavior and xenophobia are due to a lack of personal development training. That is why we encourage you to spread personal development, as it is one of the most effective ways to develop human consciousness.

I conducted a survey to understand the effects of a political conflict on African leaders and their respective communities in the U.S. At the end of the study, I discovered individuals might have had the same negative experiences during the civil war but their responses to the challenges were different. The feeling of sadness and anger was the same after losing a loved one in the civil war, but some decided to move on and others were stuck in resentment for several years.

In my studies, I came across work done by Ken Wilber, an American developmental psychologist, on the levels of consciousness. His work enlightened me with the understanding that people were at different levels of consciousness, and therefore their responses to the challenges of life differ according to their level. Wilber classified consciousness into four levels: egocentric, ethnocentric, worldcentric and cosmocentric. The level of consciousness is not only expressed at the individual level alone but also at a collective one. A community can be stuck at an ethnocentric level and not be able to move to a higher level. A leader with a higher level of consciousness can help his people move from one level to another. That is why educated leaders with broad minds and positive experiences are more than ever needed in the world. In other words, a leader must integrate cognitive knowledge and experiential knowledge to lead his people to a higher level of consciousness. This can be done through personal development.

Authors in the field of personal development agree that growth and development have a direction. It is a dynamic process toward maturity. Stephen R. Covey explained that effectiveness is to move from a dependent mindset to an independent one so that one can engage in interdependency. Growing is gradually moving toward a stage of maturity. There seems to be a visible pattern of growth in the universe. Birth, growth, death and rebirth seem to be that pattern. Developmental psychology highly supports this theory.

The emergence of developmental psychology goes back to the English psychologist William T. Preyer in 1882. In his book, *The Mind of the Child*, he explained through a rigorous scientific method the development of his own daughter from birth to two and half years. Later, empirical studies were conducted in Europe and in North America in the field of developmental psychology. Key scholars such as Jean Piaget (1896-1980), Lev Vygotsky (1896-1934) and John Bowlby (1907-1990) looked at how children develop intellectually throughout the course of their lives. Other authors, such as Lawrence Kohlberg, described stages of moral development. Saint Teresa of Avila's description of the mansions in the journey to God was a great contribution in spiritual development, as was James W. Fowler's explanation of the different stages of faith development. Additionally, Abraham Maslow's hierarchy of needs helps us to understand the psycho-social development of human beings. These authors and many others differ in the way their present their levels, but the main point is that growth or development seems to have a clear direction. Growth and development are dynamic and can be observed through human behavior.

The principles of personal development in this book came from one major book, the *Divine Principle*, and are backed up with many supportive documents from a variety of sources. I did not invent these principles. I did not create them; they already existed and were mentioned in books that I have read. However, I have tested them in my personal and professional life, and the results were incredibly positive. The application of these principles in your life will make you a new person, more aware of yourself and more conscious of your relationships. It is a constant practice and if you do not give up you will be surprised by how much you have matured as time goes by.

Personal development in general education

Nelson Mandela said, "Education is the most powerful weapon that you can use to change the world." Indeed, education is the key to eliminating gender inequalities, reducing poverty, and creating peace and sustainable development. In a knowledge-based economy, education is the new currency through which nations maintain economic competitiveness and global prosperity. Education is an investment, and it is one of the most critical investments we can make not only for ourselves but also for the larger society. This is true not only for the United States, but for every country in the world.

Students and graduates must be prepared for the real demands of the job market in a complex and ever-changing society. The holistic goal of education is to go beyond discipline-specific knowledge to facilitate the development of intellectual, emotional, social and spiritual intelligence. Preparation for entry into the job market must include development of the individual as a whole person. Unfortunately, personal development is not a subject taught in schools or universities. This kind of training should start in our early years in school and continue until adulthood, especially when we enter the job market. Every age needs mature leaders capable of resolving societal problems in a responsible manner. The school system can contribute in preparing such leaders.

Since the 1990s, the Université Félix Houphouët-Boigny has faced unprecedented crises, expressed in constant violent protests, which have created a difficult environment for learning. Despite the efforts of the authorities over the years, they have not yet found an effective solution to this violence in the university setting and the larger society. In addition, the French Development Agency, in its recent CREMID / AFD report dating from January 2019, affirmed that 80% of the graduates from Ivory Coast universities, more precisely the Université Félix Houphouët-Boigny, do not have skills that match or connect to the job market. There is a need to bring into the curriculum a program that could help resolve both the issue of violence and also the unemployment rate.

On November 10, 1998, resolution A / RES / 53/25 of the United Nations General Assembly unanimously adopted the decade 2001-2010 as the "International Decade for a Culture of Peace and Non-Violence for the Children of the World." Member states were urged to take the necessary measures "to ensure that the practice of peace and non-violence is taught at all levels of their respective societies, including in educational institutions." Unfortunately, 20 years has passed now, but this measure has not yet been implemented. Certainly, there was no concrete proposal on which decision makers could base policy changes in education programs.

This personal development training program that I have designed serves as an educational measure by providing students with the knowledge and necessary skills to become effective leaders capable of resolving conflicts in a pluralistic society. In addition, students acquire leadership and management skills considered necessary for the labor market in Africa and elsewhere in the world. More than ever, self-awareness, self-confidence, emotional, social and spiritual intelligence will be highly valued as elements of success in the 21st century.

On a societal level, Ivory Coast is experiencing difficulties in the field of human development. According to the World Bank, in 2018 the country was ranked 170th out of 189 countries according to the United Nations Human Development Index. Between 1985 and 2011, the level of poverty increased considerably, and the proportion of the poor population increased from 10% to 51%. However, the results of the latest living standards monitoring survey indicate that recent economic progress has "reduced the poverty rate to 46%." A recent report by Ms. Akin Olugbadé, Deputy Director General of the African Development Bank, explained that a cumulative share of the unemployed and vulnerable people in the workforce in Ivory Coast is in the range of 70% to 90%. More than half the job seekers in Ivory Coast have graduated from universities and colleges. In addition, Ivory Coast has suffered greatly from recurrent conflicts since the 1990s. The hope of all Ivorians is to find lasting social peace, the only guarantee to consolidate the economic development gains achieved in the country.

To address these crucial issues, it is essential that personal development training be an integral part of the educational programs at universities, colleges and even high schools. This will not only improve student success but also lay the foundation for success in entrepreneurship, leadership and management. In 2017, I was invited to teach personal development at the Université Félix Houphouët-Boigny in Ivory Coast. As this university is my alma mater, I reflected on the difficulties and challenges I went through as a student there, and this motivated me even more to offer my contribution to the university. It was my way of encouraging and giving hope to current students, whom I consider to be the leaders of the emerging Ivory Coast and Africa. There was no doubt that they needed mentors and models who could inspire and empower them to make a difference in the larger society.

The objectives of the personal development training program are to develop students' self-awareness. By knowing their strengths and limitations, they will develop wisdom to make better personal and career choices. The program is important to begin from high school so that the child knows his passion and so is able to make choices that allow him to excel and become a genius in his field. Choosing a career for a salary is not necessarily bad, but not always fulfilling. A good passion-oriented choice develops personal motivation, creativity and innovation.

The personal development training provides skills that allow you to better manage emotions by exploring emotional, social and spiritual intelligence; to practice active listening in order to better manage interpersonal conflicts; to overcome the fear of failure and to express yourself better in public in order to influence your audience. You learn how to set clear and realistic goals to maximize success; to understand the importance of teamwork in order to achieve a common goal. Also, you learn general techniques of self-management (health, time, finances and so forth).

At the end of the training program, we evaluate and measure outcomes and keep improving. Continuous improvement is key to personal and professional development. One must always remain open to constructive criticism and suggestions in order to continue improving in any training program. The goal is to integrate personal development training in elementary school through high school. When students are exposed at a younger age the chance of success is higher. Therefore, when they go to college or university, they are already prepared to make necessary changes according to their own reality.

Chapter 2: History and overview of Personal Development

Even though personal development seems to be unknown in academia it is not a new field of knowledge. Philosophers, psychologists and theologians have studied personal development since ancient times. Philosophers such as Socrates, Plato and Epicurus, as well as saints including Buddha, Jesus and Gandhi, have either consciously or unconsciously taught the ideas of personal development. Their teaching became the foundation for many experts in personal development today.

Personal development's primary focus is self-awareness. Naturally, it empowers a person to think that they can achieve what they truly believe by overcoming all kinds of obstacles. French psychologist and pharmacist, Émile Coué, is one of the pioneers in personal development. His work consisted of "self-improvement through optimistic self-talk and autosuggestion." This approach became increasingly popular from the 1920s to contemporary times.

In the postmodern era, many people recognize the concepts of positive thinking. Positive mantras or affirmations can have a wonderful effect on people and boost their level of self-confidence. This is recognized as a powerful tool to reach specific goals and be resilient in difficult times.

In the past two decades, personal development has become a major emphasis in the business world. In a fast, changing and complex global world, there is a need to approach success from an integrated perspective. Success can no longer be defined just from an economic standpoint alone. Having a sense of fulfillment, or realizing that we are living a meaningful life, is highly valued in today's world. Obviously, a truly successful life implies a balance between economic and overall wellbeing. Collaborating with others, and examining and exploring the overall well-being of people, is fundamentally essential for living a happy life. In this context, personal development becomes the foundation for effective success in leadership, in business, entrepreneurship and professional life.

Personal development can be viewed as the invisible part of an iceberg. When personal development work is done effectively, it affects all other areas of life, such as health, relationships and professional success. In that sense, we do not just appear successful, while hiding our weaknesses and challenges and pretending that all is good. We are authentic, real and true with ourselves and those we work with.

In 2006, the movie "The Secret," by Bob Proctor and Jack Canfield and written by Rhonda Byrnes, exploded the popular consciousness on the importance of personal development. This movie was viewed by more than 250,000,000 people across the globe. Since then, the term the

"Law of Attraction" has become popular in the United States and around the world.

Prior to the "The Secret," American author Wallace D. Wattles (1860 – 1911) wrote the classic book on personal development in 1910 called *The Science of Getting Rich*, which fosters the idea that changing one's way of life and habits can lead to wealth. Later, in 1937, Napoleon Hill (1883-1970) wrote *Think and Grow Rich* based on 25 years study of the 500 wealthiest people in America at the time. Napoleon Hill's encounter with Andrew Carnegie, one of the wealthiest men of his time, was a turning point in the history of personal development and the philosophy of success. Carnegie challenged Hill to work on a project which consisted of interviewing the wealthiest people. Hill was about to decline the suggestion due to lack of confidence in himself. However, he was influenced by Carnegie to make a positive move in the right direction. Since then, the growing interest in personal development has been unstoppable. Dale Carnegie's *How to Win Friends and Influence People*, published in 1936, has more than 50 million copies sold. Norman Vincent Peale's *The Power of Positive Thinking*, published in 1952, was a best seller for more than 10 years on the *New York Times* list.

One cannot ignore the massive work of Abraham Maslow and Carl Rogers who described human psychological needs from a hierarchical perspective. The need for care and love, to be acknowledged and appreciated by others, but also the need to feel fulfilled are essential for personal development.

This volume is a contribution to the field of success in personal and professional life. Implicitly, I do not separate personal from family, which I believe are tightly connected. Many sociologists support the thesis that the family is the cornerstone of society. How you grow up significantly impacts not only your personal life, but also your responsibilities as a spouse or parent are strictly linked to your individual development as a person.

In the following chapters, we will examine the fundamental question of personal identity, which is essential for self-knowledge and personal growth. The four dimensions of life, namely, the physical, the emotional, the mental and the spiritual, will be explored in purpose to identify personal gifts and callings. In addition, there will be an emphasis on how to achieve important life goals. Lastly, the focus will be on understanding universal principles and, more specifically, their application to success in personal and professional life.

Definition of terms

1. Persona

Carl Jung refers to "persona" as ego. Thomas Merton refers to it as the subjective identity of the false self. It is like the vehicle, not the driver of the dream, not the dreamer. The word "persona" is derived from the Latin word for mask. In the theaters of ancient Greece and Rome actors would wear a mask to play their role (parent, child, warrior, etc.). According to Carl Jung, the persona refers to the role people play in society. The persona is intrinsically linked to ego, as we tend to identify who we are by the role we play in society. For example, your behavior in meeting with your boss is different from when you are meeting your friends or family members for a meal.

In addition, your persona is your outer self and plays the same role as your thoughts, emotions, and body movements, and is different from your inner self, which is your consciousness, your identity. In fact, the persona also hides a dark side, built up since childhood from such things as unresolved wounds, fear of failure, rejection, and punishment from parents and society. Therefore, throughout adulthood we adopt protective, defensive attitudes and appear to be good or pretend to be good. For example, we choose makeup, hairstyle, the way we speak, our posture, all like a mask we consciously or unconsciously wear to express our ego. Even the type of car we choose to drive, where to live, and our community and organizational affiliations are aspects of our persona.

The reason why we easily become defensive has to do with the importance of being right and proving someone else wrong. In actual fact, we can stand for an idea and disagree without being overly defensive. The reality is we will always see life differently because of our subjective nature, which is influenced by gender, environment, education, culture, tradition, religious beliefs, political ideologies and so on. These factors can also become an ego-trip when we identify with them instead of experiencing our conscious self-identity.

The persona cannot do justice to the individuality of the person hiding behind it. The persona adapts to social life and responsibilities. Therefore, it is shaped through collective social forces such as peers, family, the media, etc. Ideally everyone should seek to achieve harmony between their self-identity and the persona. Normally the healthy persona can adapt to the different roles he/she plays in their lifetime. For example, a tough coach in body building can be an effective persona, especially when the exercise involves competition. However, if a similar tough persona is applied when dealing with wife and children at home it will be ineffective. In fact, we do not compete with our kids, we want the best for them. We can even accept to lose in order for them to rise. Anyone who has a family knows that one cannot convince an angry wife with philosophical arguments. A persona which can be flexible and connected with one's unique gifts, abilities, and interests can set the foundation for personal and professional success.

2. Development

Michael A. Veseth, Director of the International Political Economy program and Professor of Economics at the

University of Puget Sound, Tacoma, Washington wrote an article titled "International Political Economy." He raised the problematic of development studies as an emerging academic discipline since the second half of the 20th century, and increasing concern about economic prosperity in the third world after decolonization. In the immediate post-war period, development economics, a branch of economics, arose out of previous studies in colonial economics. By the 1960s, an increasing number of development economists felt that economics alone could not fully address issues such as political effectiveness and educational provisions. Development studies arose as a result of this, initially aiming to integrate ideas of politics and economics. Since then, it has become an increasingly inter- and multi-disciplinary subject, encompassing a variety of social scientific fields.

Nobel Prize–winning economist Amartya Sen has challenged the traditional view of development, which has focused mostly on economic growth over the past century. Traditional welfare economics focused on income as the main criterion of well-being. By the 1980s, Sen's work showed that poverty was not a matter of income alone but also involved a wider range of deprivations in health, education and living standards. He suggested the "Capability Approach," which was adapted into the UN Human Development Index, and subsequently the Multidimensional Poverty Index. The purpose was to measure development from a broader perspective. Then, in 1999, Sen went further by making the point "that freedoms constitute not only the means but the ends in development," which has also been widely accepted today.

Development must include many other aspects of human life, not only changes in people's income but more generally in terms of their choices, capabilities and freedoms. We should be concerned about the distribution of these features, not just the simple income average for a society. Development should include positive and lasting change in people's lives, providing a person not only with necessary education that could improve their overall well-being, but also with tools that can sustain growth.

On September 25, 2015, the United Nations adopted the new sustainable development agenda that aimed to end poverty, protect the planet and ensure prosperity for all by 2030. An ambitious project? One cannot effectively tackle the goal of attaining peace and social justice without putting human development at the center of the process. Among the seventeen goals, which are equally essential, human development remains the central point.

President Obama, in one of his addresses in Ghana in August 2009, said, "Africa does not need strongmen, it needs strong institutions." From an institutional perspective, it is true that Africa needs strong institutions; but Africa also needs strong peacemakers, such as Mandela, to build those institutions. One cannot be done without the other. Therefore, leadership and human development should be a key component in the pursuit of peace, social justice and long-term development. In fact, immature and egocentric leaders will make poor decisions and violate basic life principles that will lead to chaos and destruction of the nation. Immature and ethnocentric leaders will not be able to build strong institutions; they are incapable of leading others towards something bigger and sustainable. Immature and egocentric leaders mostly end up abusing power and creating conflict and even war in their nations.

By using the term "strongmen," Obama was certainly referring to those who try to obtain power and use it improperly, refuting basic democratic values or principles such as the alternation of power, human rights, and the rule of law. Any leader who rejects and violates basic human rights and women's rights, and rejects capitalism and the free market as the way to create prosperity for all has not grown up. These values are mostly rejected by the so-called "strongmen" because they consider them as western values. However, democratic values are built on universal principles and they do not belong to a culture or race. Therefore, the focus should be the development of the people so that they can integrate universal principles in their leadership style. However, what is being developed is not just the intellect, but the self, which is also referred to as consciousness.

3. Consciousness

Developmental psychologists have identified numerous features of an individual's consciousness, such as cognition (what one is aware of), values (what one considers most important), and self-identity (what one identifies with). These features of consciousness develop through recognizable stages, each stage revealing a markedly different understanding of the world. This term consciousness derives from the Latin "consciente," a word that is composed from "con" (with, having, possessing) and "scire" (to know).

In his book *Structural Phenomenology: An Empirically Based Model of Consciousness*, Steven Ravett Brown explains consciousness as a "self-conscious being," "cu-scire": with knowing, comprehension and vision. Consciousness is the "evolved, conscious, sentient being" or, better said, this is what it would be if it were formed, complete, and therefore evolved. But consciousness, usually, is still evolving, moving towards self-consciousness, also known as self-realization.

Consciousness can mean different things to different people. Even though there is no universal agreement on the definition, there is a core meaning that can integrate all other thoughts. According to Brown, the term "consciousness," however, refers to experience itself. Rather than being exemplified by a thing that we observe or experience, it is exemplified by all the things that we observe or experience. Something happens when we are conscious that does not happen when we are not conscious — and something happens when we are conscious of something that does not happen when we are not conscious of that thing. We know what it is like to be conscious when we are awake as opposed to not being conscious when in dreamless sleep. We also know what it is like to be conscious of something (when awake or dreaming) as opposed to not being conscious of that thing.

This everyday understanding of consciousness based on the presence or absence of experienced phenomena provides a simple place to start. A person, or other entity, is conscious if they experience something; conversely, if a person or entity experiences nothing they are not conscious. Elaborating slightly, we can say that when consciousness is present, phenomenal content (consciousness of something) is present. Conversely, when phenomenal content is absent, consciousness is absent. There is no real development without development of consciousness. In this context one can summarize development of consciousness as growing, evolving and improving through life experience.

Chapter 3: The inward journey of self-knowledge

How do I know myself?

1. Am I my body?

Anything that is finite is not the conscious self. Our true value is eternal, absolute, unchanging and unique. For example, when you look a person what you see first is his body. When I think I am my body, it becomes my primary preoccupation. I take care of my body more than anything else. I want this body to be perfect, so I get rid of any wrinkles, and put on a lot of makeup. When someone say you are beautiful you are so happy, even if it was only flattery. When someone is honest with you that your nose is too big, you get mad and fight that person. Some will go so far as to have plastic surgery to become perfect externally, but sooner or later they become depressed seeing their body is getting old and dying. This reminds me of the story of Narcissus, a young man who excessively loved his image to the point that he spent the whole day watching his beauty reflected in the well. One day he felt into the well and drowned.

The lesson is if you love your external body too much you might end up putting more value on the things that can satisfy only your body, such as food, expensive clothing, expensive material things such as cars, watches, shoes, etc., so that people can praise you. If this becomes your primary preoccupation, you will certainly miss the point of life as a whole. Is life about food or clothing or money? As Eckhart

Tolle said in his book, *The Power of Now*, of course, when you do not possess these external things, they are the most important, but when you possess them you will know that they are not enough for a fulfilling and happy life.

Nowadays, many young people get depressed because their photo on Facebook or Instagram has not received enough likes. They can easily develop a sense of low self-esteem. A person can have a nice body and have a nasty character. It is like a beautiful flower that smells bad. Beauty is not just external; it is also internal. That is why you should not fool yourself into thinking you are just your body. Your body will perish one day for sure. It is only a vehicle to achieve your goal; it is not your goal.

2. Am I my thoughts?

Lao Tzu, the ancient Chinese philosopher and founder of Taoism, said:

> Be careful with your thoughts because your thoughts become your words. Be careful with your words because your words become your actions. Be careful with your actions because your actions become your behaviors. Be careful with your behaviors because your behaviors become your habits. Be careful with your habits because your habits become your character. And be careful with

your character because your character becomes your destiny.

The main cause of stress is excessive thinking. Most people are so addicted to their own thoughts that they can get into useless conflict when someone else disagrees with them. For example, in American politics, liberals and conservatives cannot agree on fundamental social issues. Both groups believe their view is morally correct and superior to the other. From the very moment you think your opinion, or belief, or ideology is morally superior, you can no longer listen well to the other. You will listen with the intent to correct, judge and convert. This is the real addiction of the American society, the excessive attitude of being right. People will ruin a relationship because they have opposite views on certain sensitive matters.

We are living in a world where everyone wants to share their opinions and very few want to listen genuinely in order to understand. Listening is also learning to be present, which means beyond thinking. Most people do not know how to go beyond thinking and be present with others. Eckhart Tolle once again stated, "You cannot be present by thinking, your thoughts are taking you in the past or in the future." In fact, you can only have an authentic experience of being in the present moment. You cannot help people heal from their pain unless you learn to be present.

When you stop identifying your true self with your thoughts, you become more peaceful. The mind always wants to be right and to prove the other wrong. The role of mind is important in an intellectual, educational context, but very limited in a relationship context. Can you convince an angry spouse about a philosophical issue, even when it is logical? Authentic relationship is the place of vulnerability, a place where we become powerless and weep together. The secret of building a healthier relationship with one's co-workers, and even enemies, is to move away from the realm of thought as we deal with challenges.

3. Am I my emotions?

Human beings go through all kinds of emotions. An emotion is a felt response to something that affects you in some way. Depending on whom you ask, emotions can either be an involuntary response to something (like a reflex) or a chosen response (like a judgment). The word emotion come from the Latin "emotus," which means disturbance. This could mean emotions were primarily perceived as coming to disturb your state of being.

In psychology, emotions have been classified into two groups: the positive and the negative ones. Emotions such as fear, anger, frustration, worries, disappointment, sadness, grief, etc., are constant in many people lives. We also experience joy, happiness, contentment, gratitude, bliss, excitement, and so forth.

Most people are controlled by their emotions. They end up acting according to how they feel now and sometimes regret their actions later. For example, if you are angry and you turn violent and hurt the person you believe who made you feel angry, you might end up regretting your actions. Your conscience will remind you that you did not act rightly.

The way to control your emotions is first to understand where they come from. Negative emotions are the result of past negative experience and negative thoughts. They keep coming to your memory and the secret is not to act on them. Notice the emotions, name them and let them go. Do not have give and take with your negative emotions. You can also choose to replace them by acting positively. The next time someone says something hurtful to you and a negative thought come to your mind, think of giving them a gift and act on it and see the result. It will transform your negative experience and thought into a positive outcome. This is not common sense of course, but it is a powerful way to control your emotions. Negative emotions are just passing by, so do not act on them; notice them and let them go! Do not hold on to them and have give and take with them. Meditation is suggested to let go of negative thoughts, so that they will not be expressed in negative emotions and negative actions.

4. "I AM" oneness

Finally, what are we left with when we become aware that we are not the body, the thoughts or emotions? It is consciousness, or the conscious mind. In psychology, the term used is "inner self" or "authentic self." Some people refer to this using the religious term "soul," or presence or spirit. Our spirit is also an integral part of "oneness," the universal consciousness. In other words, our conscious self is an integral part of the universal consciousness or oneness. Most people would like to understand this through reason, but it is only experiential. You cannot explain it, and unless you experience it you really do not know what it is. That is why we encourage experiential knowledge over cognitive knowledge in the pursuit of self-consciousness.

When you experience oneness, which usually is a mystical or spiritual phenomenon, you are no longer the same. People around you can see the change in you through your presence and your way of being. Have you ever met people and while around them you were suddenly overwhelmed with a sense of inner peace, joy and serenity? If yes, you met the oneness. Even when you die, you continue to live because you keep influencing the world. That is what the Bible refers to as living for eternity. Jesus Christ died physically but continues to live in humanity's consciousness from generation to generation.

Experiencing oneness in not an intellectual exercise; it is a spiritual experience. People who have experienced oneness tend to give less value to the material world. They withdraw from the world and the established system, which drives people into buying and spending money on expensive clothing, cars and houses. They would rather spend their money to feed those in need, or invest in hospitals and education where it is needed. They become less concerned about building their own tower of Babel and more concerned with the pain of the world. They invest in humanitarian work. They seek humility, and do not need to be praised to be happy. They do not think that they are morally superior to others. They do not think in terms of black and white because they know that issues have a more complex reality than the way they appear to be. They do not automatically classify the world into those who are bad versus those who are good, and try to get rid of the bad. As Christ said in Matthew 5:45 "He causes his sun to rise on the evil and the good and sends rain on the righteous and the unrighteous." If God allows both evil and good to exist there might be a reason for that. There is a time for everything, as it says in Ecclesiastes.

People who experience oneness value honesty and live with integrity. They do not abuse power and do not need to use violence to subdue others. They relate with others based on their essence, not based on such characteristics as race, religion, ethnicity, social rank or title. They are responsible for their choices and have the courage to apologize whenever they make a mistake. They allow other people to make their own choices and encourage them to learn and grow from them. They are happy because they find deeper meaning in their existence. They do not get attached to material things and can let go of titles and positions when necessary. They seek peace with others and practice non-violence as the way to resolve conflict.

The Sufi poet Rumi, also known as Shams Tabrizi, guided us towards experiencing oneness through these words:

> If you get angry again, your struggle with yourself is not over yet.
> If you are still hurt, the roof of the house that is your heart is not yet strengthened.
> If you are still critical, your thoughts are not yet clear enough.
> If you still don't love for nothing and without making a difference,
> It is that you always use your reason and your mind and that prevents the Love which is in you from expanding.
> If you still don't give up on saying "I" Your will is always under control and is subject to your ego.
> And if you're still complaining, it's because you can't see the Divine Reality.

In conclusion, the purpose of life is to experience oneness, which is what I believe Buddhists refer to as nirvana, Christians call perfection or being Christlike, Muslims regard as when humanity completely surrenders to the will of God, and Unificationists describe as mind-body unity. This is what every human being consciously or unconsciously aspires to.

That is why we admire people such Gandhi, Christ, Muhammad, Rev. Moon, Mother Teresa, Nelson Mandela, etc. They are people who have certainly experienced oneness in their lives.

5. God is Oneness

The biggest mistake of our modern civilization comes from the idea that God was outside of ourselves. That is where the whole concept of the old white man sitting on His throne and watching us from heaven came from. First, He is male; second, He is white with white; third He has a white beard; and fourth, He is watching you from above for any mistake you make so that you are punished for it. You wonder why there are so many atheists in the western world these days! Who can trust such a God? Can you have an intimate relationship with a being like that? It is impossible unless you are okay with staying in an abusive relationship.

If God is love and is in a relationship with his creation, then He experiences human suffering as well as rejoicing with His creation. On that same line, God is not just all powerful but also all vulnerable. The idea of a God sitting on His throne and watching His creation is known in theological terms as anthropomorphism. It consists of giving God a human form and worshiping that form. In Islam, for example, anthropomorphism is rejected to avoid idolatry. Another danger of giving God a form is that we can fall into the temptation of worshiping that image instead of finding the immanent God; the presence, the omnipresence in us and around us.

God as a transcendent being naturally guides our lives, and we can only surrender to Him, her or it. The problem with western culture is that this transcendence became an object of intellectual study since the Age of Enlightenment (also known as the Age of Reason), the intellectual and philosophical movement that dominated the world of ideas in Europe during the 17th to 19th centuries and spread across the world. Reason was highly valued to the point that God became an object of study. We certainly thought we could grasp God with reason. Unfortunately, in many cases it led to spiritual arrogance, which consists of thinking that one knows God better than the other, so we could even impose that idea on others. This led to countless arguments and counter-arguments in the theological world. It even contributed to the divisions within Christianity and later Islam.

The mystery in revelation is beyond the mind; it lies in the realm of consciousness. That is why whenever we think we know God with our mind, God reveals another dimension of Himself or Herself to us; so, we never finish knowing God as a transcendent being. God keeps unfolding His different dimensions until we surrender to Him. That might be the reason why Islam means to surrender to His will. God will keep revealing Himself to us and we will never finish knowing Him. Therefore, the intellectual pursuit of God with the intent to scientifically know Him is in vain. We must surrender to his will. Whatever happens in our life that we could not control, our attitude should be like Jesus' prayer in the Garden of gethsemane: "Your will be done not mine."

Even though God is one, He expresses Himself through His creation in unique ways. This should not be confused with Hinduism, which does not emphasize the sprit self. In Hinduism, God is in everything so when an individual dies, their spirit self dissolves into the transcendence. The personal development perspective aligns with *Divine Principle,* written by Sun Myung Moon, that every being has a unique existence and a unique spirit self or conscious self, and can manifest itself through a certain form even after death. Having an experience with Jesus Christ, for example, is common as the sprit self of Christ is manifested in a form to give a message, to inspire, to heal, to guide or to show love.

6. A spiritual experience

When I was a little boy, I was very attached to my grandmother. She died when I was about five years old. At that time, I had very little understanding of death. Somehow God hides death from children for a good reason. So, my grandmother died, and I asked where she was as I had not seen her for few days. My dad said she went on a long trip and she will come back one day. One night I went to use the bathroom, and on my way back from the bathroom to go back to sleep, I saw my grandmother on her couch, smiling and asking me to come and hug her and sleep on the couch near her. I was very surprised and happy and hugged her and slept by her. It was a real experience.

In the morning, my dad came and woke me up and asked, "Why are you sleeping on grandmother's couch? Do you miss her?" I told him that grandmother told me to come and sleep with her last night. She was here. My dad replied, "You had a dream." I replied to my dad that it was not a dream, but I had seen and hugged grandmother last night. He smiled again and said it was a dream. Later that day, I shared my experience with my siblings and they all looked at each other and said, "You were dreaming." Many years after studying spirituality in depth, I realized that it was my grandmother's spirit self that had visited me and it was not a dream.

The spirit self is part of God but keeps it uniqueness and will come as a form to us on earth for a special message, or even to show us love, care and protection. God is present within us and around us!!! God is omnipresent, so every face I see is also the face of God!!! God put a part of Himself in all of us so that we can experience His unique expression. That is probably why we are called His children. Even when we die, God still allows our uniqueness to be expressed from His eternal oneness. When Jesus or Muhammad or a loved one in the spirit world appear to you, it is also God coming to you with a special message. As the Divine Principle explains so clearly:

After we shed the physical self, we enter the spirit world and live there for eternity. The reason we desire an eternal life is because our innermost self is the spirit self which has an eternal nature. Our spirit self consists of the dual characteristics of spirit mind (subject partner) and spirit body (object partner). The spirit mind is the center of the spirit self, and it is where God dwells.

In Judaism the name of God is not pronounced. Exodus 20:7 says, "Thou shalt not take the name of the Lord thy God in vain; for the Lord will not hold him guiltless that take his name in vain." This is not just about repeating the word "Yahweh" for no reason. It has a deeper meaning than that. The reason why Jewish scholars removed the vowels from "Yahweh" so that no one is able pronounce the name of God says a lot about the kind of relationship we should have with God. Have you ever tried to pronounce YHWH? You know it is impossible to do it using your tongue and your lips. If you insist on trying to pronounce YHWH, it will sound like imitating breathing, like exhaling and inhaling.

What if God's name was "breathing in and breathing out"? What if God was the breath that Adam received to make him a living being? What does a newborn do first? Inhale and exhale. What is the last thing we do before leaving this world? We inhale and exhale. What does every living being do every single moment? It is exhaling and inhaling. In fact, there is no

Islamic way of breathing, no Jewish way of breathing, no Christian or Buddhist or Hindu way of breathing; there no American or African, Japanese or Korean way of breathing. Inhaling and exhaling is universal. YHWH made Himself available to all and for all.

No religion or race or nationality can control or possess God. Richard Rohr, in his book *The Naked Now: Learning to See as the Mystics See*, wrote:

> Just keep breathing consciously in this way and you will know that you are connected to humanity from cavemen to cosmonauts, to the entire animal world, and even to the trees and the plants. And we are now told that the atoms we breathe are physically the same as the stardust from the original Big Bang. Oneness is no longer merely vague mystical notion, but a scientific fact.

PART II: The Five Principles of Personal Development

General presentation

Stages of development and principles

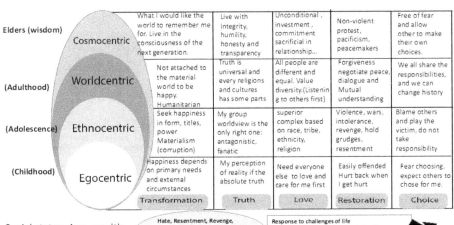

		Transformation	Truth	Love	Restoration	Choice
Elders (wisdom)	Cosmocentric	What I would like the world to remember me for. Live in the consciousness of the next generation.	Live with Integrity, humility, honesty and transparency	Unconditional, investment, commitment sacrificial in relationship...	Non-violent protest, pacificism, peacemakers	Free of fear and allow other to make their own choices.
(Adulthood)	Worldcentric	Not attached to the material world to be happy. Humanitarian	Truth is universal and every religions and cultures has some parts	All people are different and equal. Value diversity.(Listening to others first)	Forgiveness negotiate peace, dialogue and Mutual understanding	We all share the responsibilities, and we can change history
(Adolescence)	Ethnocentric	Seek happiness in form, titles, power Materialism (corruption)	My group worldview is the only right one: antagonistic, fanatic	superior complex based on race, tribe, ethnicity, religion	Violence, wars, intolerance, revenge, hold grudges, resentment	Blame others and play the victim, do not take responsibility
(Childhood)	Egocentric	Happiness depends on primary needs and external circumstances	My perception of reality if the absolute truth	Need everyone else to love and care for me first	Easily offended Hurt back when I get hurt	Fear choosing, expect others to chose for me.

Social status, Age, wealth Titles, Degree do not determine a higher level of consciousness

Hate, Resentment, Revenge, Anger, Fear, Aggressive, Abusive, Luck of trust...signs of immaturity

Response to challenges of life
1. Blame, Attack, complain, victimhood
2. Introspection, self-reflection, lessons learned
3. Self-criticism, Self-control...

The above table summarizes the different level of consciousness, the five principles, how people perceive reality and behave. Additionally, how someone, or a group of people, moves from one level of consciousness to another is explained. This table presents a general theory that helps us to understand the overall picture of the principles of personal development.

It is obvious that the body grows from childhood to adulthood. However, the growth of consciousness is visible only through observable human behavior. Ken Wilber classifies levels of consciousness into four stages: the egocentric, the ethnocentric, the worldcentric and the cosmocentric. For example, it is normal for a child to be egocentric, but not for an adult. An egocentric adult has missed something in their spiritual and emotional development.

There are 5 basic principles, which when practiced can help us move from one level to another. They are the principles of transformation, truth, love, restoration and choice. These principles are all interrelated. However, one can have a worldcentric consciousness and be ethnocentric in truth and egocentric in restoration and cosmocentric in choice. Even those who are considered as saints have some weaknesses in certain areas of growth. When we study the lives of the saints, shortcomings in certain areas of their lives are always there. Additionally, someone can have a good social status, a leadership role, a role in a family, tribe or community and still be egocentric or ethnocentric. Some people have encountered difficult childhoods, such as abuse or absence of parents, and could not overcome their difficulties so they end up dwelling in hatred, resentment, constant fear and violence toward others. The theory suggests that growth happens when our response to the challenges of life involves self-reflection, introspection and learning lessons. However, people get stuck when they always blame others, attack, and play the victim when challenges arise.

This is still an area of ongoing research and data is being collected to test these principles. Additionally, when someone becomes aware of their level of consciousness and takes a personal development course for a full semester, we can measure their growth and development in certain areas. We can also measure the growth in an organization whose members take the course by comparing the results of a pretest and posttest.

Culture and principles

Personal development works when culture is aligned with principles. What is a principle? It is a natural law. Culture is a worldview, a way of life. Our worldview is basically constructed on what we were taught growing up, and then later our experiences add to it. Our perspective is made of core convictions, which establish our viewpoint. That perception of reality is the observation of life through this filter of core convictions. Our perceptions of reality result in beliefs about right and wrong, responsibilities, values that we assume to be true and important. In fact, only the principles are true, universal, eternal, absolute and self-evident, not culture. Principles, such as the law of gravity for example, apply across all cultures.

Culture involves rituals, symbols and sometimes-false beliefs, also called assumptions. An example of an assumption is, if you want to be happy find a partner you love. This is a big assumption and can become a big delusion. Many young people are trapped in this false assumption and end up regretting their choices. The truth is, if you want to grow, get into a meaningful relationship. If you pay the price of growth you will eventually be happy. Mature people are naturally happy, because the negative external circumstances do not drive their inner state and decision making. They make the right choices based on principles. In traditional African society, for example, sacrificing a chicken and dropping its blood on stone means it will bring you good luck. But this belief is cultural, not a principle. It will not happen unless you pay the price to work hard to achieve your goals. That is aligning your culture to principles. It is not the American or European culture that makes America great, but the principles that go along with it. Africans do not need to copy another culture. They need to align their culture with principles.

Two people can attend the same church, and pray and worship the same way. One could be successful in their life because he or she knows the principles and practices them well. However, the other will fail because they do not know and practice principles. Putting on some special perfume believing it will bring you special luck is a cultural norm, but the principle behind it is to remain positive and never give up when you face hardships. You will sooner or later get lucky and have what you want, because you did not give up on what your heart truly desires.

Culture makes you feel safe, protected, providing you with a sense of belonging to a community, to a nation, to a religion. All cultures are socially constructed to give meaning to life. Each cultural group tends to emphasize identity superiority. As a result, cultural diversity becomes a challenge, with the potential for conflict. Amid cultural diversity, only universal principles can sustain different groups together. Why are there so many different cultures? Because as parts of human expression in the eyes of the Creator, known as oneness, all cultures are equally valid. All cultures carry some good aspects and some bad ones. Any cultural norm that violates the fundamental principles of life is bad, and not helpful. Therefore, you are free to embrace the culture of your choice. But, align your culture with the principles of growth in order to experience success in your personal and professional life.

Reflection questions

1. Name an assumption / a popular belief in your culture, ethnic group or religion. And what would be the universal principle underlying this hypothesis or belief?

2. What principle enables us to establish strong and lasting bonds with those who are different from us (ethnically, religiously, politically, racially, etc.)?

3. What is the difference between culture and principle? Give an example in a professional context.

4. Do you know any role models who have demonstrated a high level of consciousness in your culture or religion, in business or politics? Cite their names and explain how they demonstrated a high level of consciousness.

5. Accepting diversity of opinions is the most important thing a leader should embody! This allows him to better lead his team. What principle supports such a claim?

6. Is there a time in your life when you have failed to practice any of these principles? Which one? And what lessons have you learned?

I. The Principle of Transformation

1. Definition and theory

The American Psychological Association defines transformation as a change in appearance, form, function or structure. It also means metamorphosis. In psychoanalytic theory, transformation is the process by which unconscious wishes or impulses are disguised in order to gain admittance to consciousness. This definition is the theoretical aspect that gives us a general idea of the word. Now let us look deeper into the principle itself.

On September 27, 1905, Albert Einstein published an article the essence of which was to explain the theory of relativity, which in fact was observable in the universe. It can be summed up in mathematical terms such as $E = mc^2$. E means *energy,* m means *matter* and c represents *the speed of light in a vacuum or time*. Time here is not chronological but rather a T moment. This principle has always governed the universe and continues to do so. In the context of personal development, the principle of transformation is what helps you make an idea a reality. Knowing this principle and applying it can produce phenomenal results in our personal and professional life.

In much simpler terms, $E = mc^2$ as a universal principle means that life energy becomes matter and matter also turns into energy over time. Everything that exists is created twice, first in the invisible domain and then in the visible domain. You can become who you want to be in this life if you apply this principle. You can achieve any goal if you apply this principle. Each of us is born for a reason. This principle is first to help you discover your vision and mission, and then to help you achieve it. We all have a gift and a hidden talent, and it is our responsibility to discover it. This principle is also the principle of leadership, not only as a social position but also as a social responsibility.

Personal development leads to knowing yourself, your potentials and your weaknesses. Then you can value teamwork to achieve a dream or a common project. To realize your vision, you must be passionate and deeply love what you want to become. Normally your personal talent should be linked to your vocation. Unfortunately, the reality of many developing countries demands that people find a job to get out of misery and poverty. However, you can be engaged in your professional life and do what you are passionate about at the same time. There is only one life, so live it fully.

Also, you need to be able to communicate your vision to the people around you. You will certainly meet people who share the same vision. So, you can create a team and establish a common vision and mission together. Remember that there is a gap between your vision and your current reality, and to bridge that gap you need a clear and realistic plan. Vision represents (invisible) energy, current reality represents (visible) matter, and time represents your plan and strategies.

There are two aspects to time. One aspect we master by seriously following our plan, and the other aspect we cannot grasp. This is the instant T during which the transformation takes place. It is impossible to observe it; one can only observe the result. Therefore, we must invest ourselves fully and leave to fate what escapes our responsibility.

The exercise below is an orientation to better know or focus your energy as a leader. No matter what type of leader you are, remember that you can choose not to follow your passion; it will be your choice. However, getting yourself oriented towards your passion is the most meaningful thing in your life. Then work will be a source of joy and happiness despite the difficulties that will arise. Working just to survive for the rest of your life is not a purpose. It is the worst life you can ever live. Go where your heart calls you, that is the meaning of this exercise. Find your unique talent and offer it to the world as a gift. Find your voice, your divine calling, and offer it to others. That is living a meaningful and joyful life.

2. What type of leader are you?

On a scale of 1 (never) to 10 (always), indicate how true the following statements are for you. Use as much of the 10-point scale as you can. Tease out differences in how often you do these things, or how true they are for you, so that you are not giving everything the same number. A "5" means average; in other words, this statement is about as true for you as it is for other people you know.

1. When doing a big task, I break it down and take it one step at a time

2. I am direct and to the point.

3. My moods go up and down.

4. I love to win.

5. I am conscientious about commitments.

6. I enjoy the energy of networking.

7. I have many stacks of papers, books, etc. around my office and home.

8. When faced with obstacles I push harder.

9. I have a hard time finding where I put things.

10. I make work fun.

11. I know how to work the system and get cooperation.

12. When people are upset, I remain calm and rational.

13. I do things in a hurry.

14. I used to daydream in school.

15. I think life is in flux, nothing is fixed.

16. I can get stuck and not know which way to move when under pressure.

17. I like to let go and see where events will lead.

18. In conflict, I fire back.

19. I'm an optimistic person.

20. I'm steady and dependable.

21. I often go back and forth on difficult decisions.

22. I come up with highly unusual ideas.

23. It is important for me to do what is expected of me.

24. If something isn't getting done fast enough then I will do it myself.

To calculate your totals for each pattern, add:

#2, 4, 8, 13, 18, and 24 for Driver: _____

Strength: Gets straight to the point
Weakness: Too competitive

#1, 5, 12, 16, 20, and 23 for Organizer: _____

Strength: Proceeds step by step and manages different tasks well
Weakness: Does things at the last minute, can miss important things in the process

#3, 6, 10, 11, 19, and 21 for Collaborator: _____

Strength: Encourages, supports and cooperates
Weakness: Spends too much time socializing

#7, 9, 14, 15, 17, and 22 for Visionary: _____

Strength: Proposes new and fresh ideas
Weakness: Not practical and does not follow through

Source: *Move to Greatness: Focusing the Four Essential Energies of a Whole and Balanced Leader* by Ginny Whitelaw and Betsy Wetzig

3. Interpretation of energies linked to types of leadership

If your highest score is the Driver, your energy is the warrior. Warriors are very often ready to take the lead in activities, to mobilize, and are ready to speak out to galvanize. They don't hesitate to take the first step and guide others towards a goal. However, the weakness of warriors as leaders is that they easily fall into internal quarrels. They love the energy of competition since they always want to win. They do not know how to handle internal conflicts. Driver leaders who are aware of their weakness surround themselves with collaborators to balance their leadership. Drivers are more successful in academia, research, teaching, journalism, judges and lawyers, military, police, and security careers. Drivers are often at the mercy of visionaries who use them to achieve their goals. Drivers can also turn against visionary leaders to fight them.

If your highest score is Organizer, your energy is service. Servant leaders are hardworking people. They invest a lot to serve others. They are meticulous; they love details. They like discipline and order. They take it step by step to better manage what they do. They are practical and reasonable. The weakness of the organizers is that they often lack a long-term vision; they do things at the last minute. Often they are successful but the job may be poorly done due to lack of long-term preparation. Organizers are more successful in careers in administration, heads of protocols, secretaries, assistants, assistant managers and spokespersons. They are also naturally good at marketing and sales, technology in general, IT, catering, human resources, finance, economic management and banking. Organizers need visionaries to help them see the long term in order to better prepare for the future.

If your highest score is Collaborator, your energy is wisdom. Collaborators are people who know how to encourage others to work together, they like teamwork and cooperation. They prefer unity, harmony between team members, and often care too much. They don't like conflict situations and always seek to appease others and prevent violence. They are great advisers, people who love spirituality. Their weakness is that they can spend too much time getting to know others. They enjoy the company of others, can listen well and often forget about time. Collaborators succeed in careers such as diplomats, religious leaders, and traditional chiefs. They are also therapists, psychologists, psychiatrists, and great mediators. If you want peace, work with collaborators; they will advocate reconciliation between people. They are also people who love humanitarian work. They are often a little too idealistic and sensitive to the suffering of the world.

If your highest score is Visionary, your energy is king. They usually have exceptional ideas, ideas that are out of the ordinary. These are people who have a vision of the future. They know how to talk about it so that they can motivate a lot of people to do amazing things. They are eloquent people with a natural charisma. Their weakness is that they are not very practical and have a hard time following up on their ideas. They are not detail oriented. That is why conscious visionaries know how to surround themselves with organizers to succeed in their mission. Visionaries succeed in careers in politics, in the business world in general, because they know how to create confidence in others, and they can motivate and create an energy around themselves to achieve something that people dream of. They can also be good entrepreneurs by creating new ideas. These are successful people as leaders of political associations, trade unions and civil society. They also know how to be activists, designer engineers, designer architects, artists and careers requiring creative ideas in general. Sometimes they do not come through and end up disappointing the people to whom they promise paradise on earth.

This exercise is about giving you an idea of where you need to orient yourself in your life mission. However, if you have any doubts, listen to your heart, trust your voice, your inner self. It is within you that lies the final answer to your life mission. Your heart, your conscience will not betray you. The exercise below is a supplement after finding out what type of leader you are. It will allow you to know the important things in your life in order to rearrange your personal and professional life. So, do it with sincerity and honesty.

4. Personal reflection

This reflection is an additional exercise to help you find your life mission. Take some time in a calm place and answer these questions. Your life mission truly starts when you can envision the end.

You attend your best friend's funeral. You have arrived at the funeral home and you see familiar faces. Everyone is sad and some people are still crying. You walk directly to the coffin to look at the body. When you look at the body you realize that it is your own body and your funeral. You turn around, you see your family members, colleagues and friends. You have just become aware of your own death.

1. Say three things you would like to hear about yourself on that day?

Answer:

....

2. Say three things that you would not want to be said about you that day?

Answer:

....

3. What would be your biggest regret?

Answer:

....

4. What would be your greatest joy?

Answer:

....

5. If you had another chance at life, what would your life be like? (Tell your life story in few words as you wish).

Answer:

....

....

....

5. Develop your vision and mission

A lot of people don't know what to do with their life. They live day to day hoping for a miracle to happen someday so that their life will become better. Without a vision of the future one can only survive, not thrive. What do you want to accomplish in the next 5 or 10 years? What does it look like (mental image)? Here there are some examples that may be relevant to your calling or life mission: Transform other people's lives through coaching in personal development; Become an international reference or an expert in the field of personal development.

A man without a vision ultimately perishes. Don't live by accident. There is a reason we have a conscience which helps human beings to see the future. No other being can do it except human beings.

How do you explain that among millions of sperms you are the only one who fertilized an egg and ended up on earth breathing and walking? Are you aware that you had more energy than all the other millions of sperms? Have you ever wondered why you were the fastest sperm? Are you here by chance or is there a reason for that?

In personal development there is no such thing as chance. You are here on earth for a very specific mission and you must play your part fully until you take your last breath. It is no accident that you were born in the year 2000, for example, and not in the same era as Jesus Christ or Muhammad (peace be upon them). And it is no coincidence that you were born in America and not in a small village in Africa. Likewise, your birth, the place of your birth and the time of your birth, is not an accident. Therefore, your life on earth is not an accident and the day of your death will not be an accident either. So, step up, listen to your voice, your inner self, and make a commitment to doing what the universe has planted in you. This is the purpose of your existence on earth.

To develop a vision and personal mission statement, first answer the following questions:

1. What problem do you want to solve?

....

2. How do you want to solve the problem?

....

3. When do you want to solve it?

....

4. Where do you want to solve it?

....

5. Who do you want to serve?

....

6. Why do you want to solve this problem?

....

7. What are your values?

....

After answering these questions, develop your mission in 30 to 35 words maximum. An example of a personal mission statement is: To integrate personal development training into the curricula of public and private universities in Africa in order to revolutionize consciousness and meet the challenge of leadership, management and entrepreneurship in Africa.

Don't rush to develop your personal mission statement. Take the time you need. When you are done, make a copy and keep it somewhere you will see it constantly. This is how the energy begins to crystallize in your consciousness. Share your mission with others, be open to feedback from others, and constantly improve yourself.

For those who want to succeed in their married life, it is also necessary to create a family mission. It is important to include all family members in the process of developing your family mission. Do not impose, do not declare, but share and be open to feedback from all members of the family so that everyone can approve it. Example of a family mission: Our family is constantly committed to practicing true love, and managing conflict through dialogue, mutual respect and forgiveness. The family mission must become the constitution of the family. All members should refer to the family constitution to resolve issues that arise in the family context.

Finally, organizations, companies and institutions must also develop a mission that includes the members of their organization. The process must also extend to the different cells of the organization by aligning the cell missions with the overall mission of the institution. An example of a company's mission is therefore: The mission of Success Consulting

Services consists of training, coaching and mentoring African youth in personal development in order to meet the challenge of leadership, management and entrepreneurship.

6. Your strategic plan

Now, between your dream and your current reality there is a gap, a void, and this void is filled with a clear and realistic plan. If you have a dream and don't have a plan, you're just a dreamer. However, if you have a plan and you execute your plan you are a leader.

The strategic plan has two essential aspects: when you are going to do what you set out to do; and how you plan to do it. This is the strategy. Also, there is a factor of time that escapes human reason. These are phenomena that we have not anticipated, such as accidents, natural disasters, and often even the death of a loved one. So, you have to adjust the plan according to the realities you face as time goes by. There are decisions that are not up to you either, for example the decision to sign a contract often depends on your client's realities and you can only wait and hope your client will make the decision. To this must be added a plan that you must follow rigorously.

An example of a strategic plan that you can use as a model in developing your own:

Time	Actions	Objective reached?	
5 years	....	yes	no
4 years	....	yes	no
3 years	....	yes	no
2 years	....	yes	no
1 year	....	yes	no
11 months	....	yes	no
10 months	....	yes	no
9 months	....	yes	no
8 months	....	yes	no

7 months	....	yes	no
6 months	....	yes	no
5 months	....	yes	no
4 months	....	yes	no
3 months	....	yes	no
2 months	....	yes	no
1 month	....	yes	no
3 weeks	....	yes	no
2 weeks	....	yes	no
1 week	....	yes	no
Today	....	**yes**	no

Every week: Make a weekly evaluation of your activities considering time management.

Every day: What actions do you take that fall within the scope of your mission? What actions do you take each day that bring you closer to your vision and your life mission? Make those activities the priority in your life. Make those activities an integral part of your daily habit.

7. Time management

We have 24 hours in a day. Most people sleep 8 hours and work 8 hours. In that case we have 8 hours left to do what we want most. However, as we are not organized, very often we spend the time doing nothing or doing things that are not at all productive. Stephen R. Covey, in his book *The 7 Habits of Highly Effective People*, explained that time management is crucial for success.

There are activities that are **urgent and important**, such as accidents, unexpected deaths, unexpected illnesses, relationship crises and natural disasters. We can control some of them, but some we cannot. Therefore, it is much better to focus on activities that are **not urgent and important**. These are the activities related to our vision, our mission, our professional life and our important relationships that we must maintain on a regular basis. These activities also include regular exercise and having fun.

❖ **Self-management in time: Classify your weekly activities according to your vision**

Urgent and Important	Not Urgent and Important
• Unanticipated activities, cases of accidents, death, illness and unscheduled emergencies • Crisis management (poorly managed relationships) • Natural disasters	• Activities related to your vision and mission (activities programmed in advance) • Activities related to your family's situation (wife, children) • Your professional life • Sport and leisure
Urgent and Not Important	**Not Urgent and Not Important**
• The expectations of others • The professional expectations of your boss, your friends, your colleagues, your family members	• Watching TV for hours • A long phone call that has nothing to do with your life mission, your goals and your vision • Spending an hour on the Internet, games, videos, social networks

Source: Stephen R. Covey

Urgent but not important activities often come from people who ask for last minute help. Depending on the relationship we have with that person, we can choose to say no or yes. That is why it is good to plan so that we are not surprised. Finally,

not urgent and not important activities must be reduced or eliminated if necessary. These are things that do not contribute to the realization of our vision and our mission. These activities are secondary or not necessary, and therefore we do not need to spend too much time on them. Examples are watching TV for hours, playing video games all day, etc.

The important thing to remember in this table is that the not urgent and important activities are activities that we need to focus on the most; they are the most important activities. When we focus on the not urgent and important things, we can use our time well and accomplish a lot in a short period of time. It is also essential to evaluate the table on a weekly basis in order to make the necessary adjustments.

8. Healthy lifestyle

Illness is one of the biggest challenges in the realization of our projects and dreams. We can have all the good ideas, the right training, but if we are in a hospital bed, we won't be able to do much. Personal development emphasizes preventative health. We do not need to wait until we get sick to go the doctor. Sometimes that is too late. If we adopt a healthy lifestyle, we can prevent many diseases and live longer. However, there are cases which fall under the mystery of life, such as accidents which one did not expect at all. You may be sitting in your front yard and a car loses control and hits you. As a result, you can die or be paralyzed. You did not cause such a situation; it is part of destiny. There are also genetic issues that are beyond us. If you were born with a genetic problem, you have less control over it as you did not choose it. Sometimes we have to learn to live with things we cannot change. However, in most cases it is possible to prevent diseases.

• **The importance of water**

A lot of people don't drink enough water. Yet, we say that water is the source of life. The planet would not exist without water. Life comes from water. Wherever there is water, there is potential for life. It is also a source of health. Water is the first and most important thing the body needs. Our body needs at least 2.5 liters of water every day. Water cleanses the kidneys and helps blood flow through the body. Blood contains 90% water, and blood carries oxygen to different parts of the body.

Without water there is no life. In fact, drinking enough water every day constitutes a choice to be healthy and to cleanse our bodily systems of all kinds of toxins and diseases.

Following are some scriptures that explain the importance of water for life, revealing that God created everything out of water:

> It is He Who created the heavens and the earth in
> six days and His Throne was on the water, so that
> He could test you, which of you is better indeed.

But if you told them, "You will indeed be resurrected after death," those who disbelieve would be sure to say, "This is nothing but obvious magic." (The Noble Qur'an 11: 7)

In the beginning God created the heavens and the earth. Now the earth was formless and empty, darkness was over the depths, and the Spirit of God was hovering over the waters. (Genesis 1:2)

Do not the disbelievers see that the heavens and the earth were reunited (as one creation unit), before they cut them into pieces? We made every living thing out of water, so believe? (The Noble Qur'an, 21:30)

It is He who created man from water: then He established lineage and marriage relationships: for your Lord has power (over all things). (The Noble Qur'an, 25:54)

And God created every animal out of water: among them there are some that crawl on their belly; some who walk on two legs; and some who walk on four. God creates what He wants. For in truth God has power over all things. (The Noble Qur'an, 24:45)

Scientifically, "protoplasm is the basis of all living matter and the vital power of protoplasm depends on the constant presence of water." (*Text-book of Botany*, by J.M. Lowson, University Tutorial Press, 1922). Zoology textbooks are also clear on this point. For example, T.J. Parker and W.A. Haswell, *Textbook of Zoology*, London, 1910, Vol I: "Living protoplasm always contains a large amount of water." In fact, the constitution of protoplasm is about 80 to 85 percent water.

About 72% of the surface of our globe is still covered with water, and it has been estimated that if the surface inequalities were all leveled, the entire surface would be underwater, as the average level of land would be 7,000-10,000 feet below the ocean surface. This shows the predominance of water on our globe.

That all life began in water is also a conclusion that our latest knowledge in the biological sciences demonstrates. Aside from the fact that protoplasm, the original basis of living matter, is liquid or semi-liquid and in a state of constant flux and instability, there is the fact that terrestrial animals, such as higher vertebrates, including humans, show, in their embryological history, organs like those of fish, indicating the aqueous origin of their original habitat.

• **Healthy food**

Sugar is part of our daily diet, but it is dangerous to eat too much sugar, especially refined sugar. Many studies inform us that the consumption of sugar promotes diabetes and obesity. Sugar also increases the level of triglycerides and cholesterol in the blood. Sugar promotes hypertension and cardiovascular disease. Recent studies tell us that sugar feeds cancerous cells. We therefore encourage you to stay away from sugar as much as possible. Sugar is a silent killer. If you're feeling overweight or still sick, ban sugar from your diet for at least 21 days. Then take it moderately.

Additionally, if you add excessive consumption of meat and too much fat, your health will gradually deteriorate. It is recommended that we eat more greens, such as salad, fruits and more fish. It is also recommended to drink less milk because we are no longer babies. Adults can survive without milk. Too much milk causes belly fat and this can be detrimental to you in the long run. In Africa, the broth known as "Maggi Cube" and its consumption leads to high blood pressure for many people. However, its consumption is so integrated in the culture that most people do not care anymore.

In fact, we can eat whatever we want from time to time, but not make it a habit. Bad and unhealthy habits gradually make us sick. Instead, we must get into the habit of eating healthy food and getting into regular exercising.

• **Physical exercise**

It is crucial to exercise at least 1 hour per day and 4 to 5 times per week. It is highly recommended to do some fast walking and running to maintain a healthy cardio and boost your immune system. The World Health Organization recommends walking 10,000 steps a day in order to burn the calories in our body. Calories come from food and when we're inactive and sitting all the time they don't burn but turn into fat in the body. Body fat then leads to all kind of heart diseases. Daily exercise lowers the cholesterol level in the blood, helps burn fat, and can naturally prevent heart disease.

An interesting fact that I observed recently is the eating habits have not changed in Ivory Coast for centuries, but the daily activities have changed and not in the right way. In the past, the main profession was agriculture, so after eating heavy foods such as foutou, placali, grape sauce, or attiéké, people walked or rode their bikes for miles to go to the farm, for their daily farm work. But today, people eat the same kinds of foods, drive their cars all the time, and sit in their desks all day. Eating habits, such as the consumption of grilled meat, called "choukouya" in Ivorian jargon, accompanied by beer or wine can in the long run be very dangerous for one's health if there is no constant exercise and physical activity. These daily habits can be the main causes of stroke and heart attack that have recently been observed in increased numbers in the country.

Calories are meant to be burned, not kept. Sport not only strengthens the immune systems but also prevents disease. So, take up the challenge of working out at least 4 times a week and improving your diet and you will see the results yourself. It is never too late; no matter your age or your weight you can adapt physical exercise accordingly. If you're having trouble getting started, sign up for a gym and find a life coach.

9. Financial management

If we shared all the wealth of the world among the 7 billion people equally, in a few years we would find ourselves in the same situation with the poor and the rich. Poverty is first a state of mind; it is our way of managing our money. Poverty is living beyond our means. Two people can have the same salary, but, depending on their standard of living, one will be financially independent and the other dependent. Many people prefer to spend on looks rather than living within their budget.

A simple exercise is to list your cash inflow and expenses. If your expenses are more than your cash inflow, you are below the poverty line no matter how much you earn. You have two options, keep your expenses as low as possible, especially non-fixed expenses such as shopping for clothes, electronics, and cash outflow. The second option is to find a second source of regular income. Sell something to earn a profit. Don't take a loan to start a business; it's too risky. Count on your own funds. Then, if your business is booming and the need for customers grows, you can take out a loan to expand your business.

Financial freedom comes from saving and investing. Poverty begins when you don't control your spending. It's not about how much you earn; it's about how much you spend. Buy only what you really need. It saves you money to start your own business. Do not take out loans to buy consumer products such as TV, cars, clothes, shoes, etc. Use credit cards to build your line of credit. However, do not go beyond your capabilities. Don't spend what you can't pay back. Wealth and financial freedom start with saving and investing, not in spending. No one gets rich by chance; it's hard work and a long-term commitment. Make sure you pay your bills on time to avoid high interest rates.

We need to organize our finances in such a way as to control spending. Then we make the conscious decision to spend what is needed at that precise moment. We live in a consumer society. Every day we are bombarded with advertisements on television to buy, buy and buy; sometimes things that are not even necessary for our life. In addition, there are many holidays for buying a gift for your loved one, and it has become such an important tradition to the point of being addictive. Ask yourself this question every time you want to spend money: Is it necessary, or is it just because I want it? Spending less takes discipline and responsibility. A lot of people could become millionaires over time if they knew how to save and invest their money.

There is no reason to say that you don't have the capital to start your business. If you make a financial plan to save $100 per month, in 5 years that is $6,000. Is it possible to start a small business with $6,000? Of course, the answer is yes. During those 5 years, you can also prepare your business plan, study the market, research clients, and attend training to strengthen your abilities. Do not be tempted to take out loans to start a business. It is too risky. Most business fail in 2 to 5 years. That is why it is better to start from your own savings. When you make it through the first years and want to grow your business you can now take out a loan.

For the past 60 years, many African countries have borrowed from the World Bank and the IMF, but this money has not been invested in creating wealth. Therefore, after 60 years most of these countries remain in debt and are unable to repay it. The IMF, World Bank, and other financial institutions are like the credit card companies in the United States. They give you high interest loans, so you never finish paying them. Africa must stop taking loans and must rely on its own wealth. Where appropriate, a loan must first go into investing and building wealth through entrepreneurship.

Taking out loans to pay salaries or to build highways and schools is not a smart way to build the economy. Africans must first rely on their national funds to build hospitals, bridges, roads, schools and pay government salaries. If corruption is reduced, then the loans will be used to create businesses and train young people in entrepreneurship so that they can generate wealth in the country. Africa's socio-economic development is directly linked to its financial independence. Expecting the European bank to always fund it is not the best way to sustain an economy. That is dependency, and no dependency leads to independence.

10. Entrepreneurship in Africa

Entrepreneurship can play an important role in Africa's economic growth, but to achieve this goal, governments, policymakers and international organizations need to focus on certain essential points. Most young people are not encouraged to engage in entrepreneurship, and when they do, the environment is not always helpful. In many African countries, political and social instabilities mostly destroy people's efforts towards entrepreneurship.

It is recommended that the spirit of entrepreneurship be integrated into the education system in Africa from primary to higher education. It should be part of the general curriculum so that every high school graduate has the skills and tools to start their own business. In addition, the bank should be able to lend money at a lower interest rate whenever an entrepreneur needs to grow their business. That means he/she has passed the first and most difficult phase. In collaboration with the private sector, the government should support the process of training and mentoring young entrepreneurs. Ideally, a successful entrepreneur could mentor other small business owners to increase their chances of success.

One of the main challenges of entrepreneurship is that most people give up. According to Jacques Leroueil, a French financial specialist, "Africa holds the prize for cessation of activity, with an average rate of 12.7%, against 6.8% in Europe, 9.6% in Latin America and 12% in North America." The mindset issue is a major factor as there is a tendency to blame others when something doesn't work out: It's always someone else's fault. This kind of mentality does not help growth and development. Those who always blame others don't learn from their own mistakes. This could be addressed effectively with training in personal development.

Learning from mistakes is normally an important factor in successful entrepreneurship. There is always a risk factor associated with doing business. Therefore, learning from the mistakes of others reduces the risk. We cannot separate personal development, leadership and entrepreneurship. What motivates someone in business has to be about their talents, gifts, and service to others. It takes personal development and leadership and a sense of responsibility.

In addition, continuing education is a major element in the success of entrepreneurship. The world is changing, new products and new delivery methods are constantly on the market. Therefore, it is important to be up to date. Many books are published every day in the field of entrepreneurship. It would be a disaster for entrepreneurs to think that they don't need continuing education in their field. The advantage of education is that we are always learning new things that help us improve our own business. We may also learn that some practices are obsolete and no longer relevant, so it is necessary to adapt to the new reality of the market.

The African continent must find concrete solutions to the difficulties it is currently going through, including massive unemployment of young people (graduates or not). Access to education, training, quality health care, electrification, and so forth will not happen without the advent of innovative ideas. Entrepreneurship alone will not suddenly change Africa but will significantly contribute to its development. Finally, no one will come to develop Africa for Africans. It's up to you and me to do it. It is our collective responsibility as Africans.

In conclusion, the principle of transformation is the principle of changing the impossible to the possible. It is making the invisible mind become the visible reality. Everything that exists physically was first thought of mentally. Everything was first in the realm of the invisible. The house, the car, the airplanes, ships and so on were all conceived in the mind first and then they became tangible, and real. Your dream is certainly in your mind, so pursue it and you will without doubt live it in the right time. If something is born in your mind and excites you, then it is achievable.

However, you need to know how to study it and work with other people to achieve your dream. Therefore, you need to master the principle of truth.

II. The Principle of Truth

1. Definition and practice

According to the *Merriam-Webster Dictionary*, truth is the body of real things, events, and facts, the state of being. From a transcendent perspective, truth is the fundamental essence or spiritual reality. Truth is also a judgment, a proposition, or an idea that is true or accepted, such as the laws of thermodynamics (transformation and conservation of energy). It is the body of true statements and propositions; the property (as of a statement) of being in accord with fact or reality; what is considered common sense. Truth is also "fidelity to an original idea or to a standard." Truth is sincerity in action, character, and utterance. These definitions are mostly theoretical. What then is the principle of truth?

In the context of personal development, truth is first of all universal. What is true is true forever; it is true for everyone; it is undeniable at all levels; and it is true not because it is a point of view but as a universal principle. The main characteristic of the principle of truth is its universality. The principle of truth does not change from place to place, from culture to culture, or from religion to religion. It can be described differently but its essence remains the same; it is universal.

That is why we must not make the mistake of wanting to possess the principle of truth intellectually. Nobody can claim the absolute truth! Every culture, every religion, every field of study perceives and describes the universal truth differently. The universal truth escapes the realm of reason. However, personal truth can be discovered if we do some introspection. To better understand the universal truth, let us refer to the story of the six blind men and the elephant, which has its origin in the Hindu tradition.

2. The six blind men and the elephant

Long ago six blind men lived in a village in India. They had no idea what an elephant looked like. Even though they couldn't see it, they told themselves they were going to try to feel it and describe it. They all went to where the elephant was and everyone tried to touch it. "Hey! The elephant is a pillar!" said the first, touching his leg. "Oh no! It's like a rope," said the second, touching his tail. "What! It's like the thick branch of a tree!" said the third, touching his trunk. The fourth said: "It's like a large fan," touching his ear. Excited and confident, the fifth exclaimed: "It's like a huge wall," touching his belly. "It looks like a horn!" said the sixth, blowing in vain, hoping for a sound and touching his tusk.

They began to argue and debate, each of them insisted on what they believed was true and that the others were wrong. They could not agree. Each blind man strongly believed he was right. A wise man was passing by and saw them arguing with each other, and he asked them: "What's going on?" "We can't agree on what the elephant looks like," they said. Each of them described their truth. The wise man said to them: "You each have some part of the truth. The reason why each one of you describes it differently is because you have touched a different part of the elephant. Yes, the elephant has all these parts you just described." The six blind men were joyfully surprised: "Oooh!" They stopped arguing and appreciated the fact that their individual realities allowed them to get a bigger idea of what an elephant looks like.

This story is a beautiful illustration of what we call the truth. In reality, we all perceive and describe part of the truth and not the whole truth. If everyone could understand this reality, there would be less violent conflict between us.

3. How to manage different perceptions of the truth

As a leader, or manager of a team, you must understand that each of your team members has a perception of the truth regarding a given subject. Each member of your team will describe the truth according to their reality, their role and responsibility in the organization, and so on. Your role is to take a step back in order to be able to bring together all these understandings of the truth to make a consensus for a common project in which everyone feels important and included. This approach is valuable in your personal, family and professional life.

It may happen that contradictory or irreconcilable positions arise sometimes concerning non-negotiable issues. In that case, you have to decide to humbly encourage the parties to let go and align for the sake of the bigger picture. If that is not possible, offer the choice to withdraw from the project. People must be free to make their own choice, even if that choice is not what we want. We need to allow them to be free. Above all, one must avoid "top down" decisions as a leader. It is very easy to fall into the temptation of imposing our perception of reality as the truth to all because of the social position we hold. This is the most dangerous approach to leadership as it will feed your ego and destroy the meaningful relationship you have with your team. So, when we are describing the truth, we have to be mindful that it is an interpretation of the truth not the truth itself. As the wise man said, we point at the moon and try to convince others that our finger is the moon. What we often call objective or ultimate truth is in most cases an interpretation of the truth and not the truth itself.

As subjective beings, each individual is a unique expression of the truth, and perceives the truth according to the spheres of consciousness: egocentrism, ethnocentrism, worldcentrism and cosmocentrism. We are all at different levels of consciousness: An ethnocentric person will not describe the truth in the same way as a worldcentered person. People perceive and describe the truth based on the social conditions, especially those expressed through the media. For example, many people believe that expensive products are good quality. Many of us have been conditioned to think like this so we can spend a little bit more. Another social condition is you will be happy when you have a lot of money. When we have money, we realize that it not true since happiness is not defined in terms of numbers alone.

Abraham Maslow, an American psychologist of the 20th century, classified human needs on four levels: The first is the primary need, that is, having to eat, drink, sleep and have sex. When you don't have your primary needs satisfied, you tend to describe reality according to those needs. Then come the needs relating to one's social security (work, car, and having a house). At this level the perception of truth is influenced by this reality. Additionally, there is the need to belong to a community, a group, in order to feel protected and loved. At this level, the perception of reality is based on our group, community, religion or ethnicity.

Finally, there is the need to serve others, to share what we have with those who need it. At this level we describe reality according to the needs of others and how it fulfills our dignity, our self-esteem. To this must be added culture, religion, education, and personal experiences. We do not have the same personal experiences. Experience shapes our reality every day. A new experience gives us a new perspective on life. We must also add gender, since women and men perceive a problem from different angles. This is all the more apparent in marriage. One of the causes of conflict in a couple has its root in the fact that men and women are fundamentally different. This is why human beings will always have a different perception of reality. This is the universal truth.

4. The origin of reason

The way most of us think has been largely influenced by Western education which originates in Cartesian thinking. French philosopher René Descartes (1596-1650) is the father of modern philosophy, which was later promoted to the Age of Enlightenment or the Age of Reason. The famous quote *"Cogito, ergo sum"* meaning "I think, therefore I am" has put an emphasis on thinking as the most valuable dimension of a human being. Other dimensions, such as human emotion and intuition, have been neglected. The human brain has a logical part, but also an emotional part and an intuitive part. Therefore, Descartes' biggest error was to reduce human ultimate value to the logical or intellectual mind.

The scientific method, or research to find out the truth, has followed a logical process. First, you make assumptions, conduct a survey and collect data, use a sample, analyze the data, draw conclusions and make recommendations. This method will certainly get you to the contextual truth but not the absolute truth. That is why scientific research allows the researcher to present the limits of the study, limits which can serve as the basis for further research in the future.

The logical mind has set the tone for intellectual debate and argument rather than genuinely seeking dialogue. In debate, one has to convince the other, whereas in dialogue it is about understanding why the other sees differently. In dialogue we can disagree and respect the other person's point of view. The dualistic mind, which always compares, contrasts, judges and condemns, has been one of the root causes of conflicts. For example, the debate over the issue of the Trinity divided the Orthodox Church and the Catholic Church in the early days of Christianity. The debate between the German theologian Martin Luther and the Catholic Church was conducted for some thirty years in Europe in the 15th century. The debate between the successors of Muhammad led to a bloodbath between Shiites and Sunnis. The debate among Europeans on the issues of militarism, imperialism and nationalism led to World War I and World War II. And the list goes on.

The logical mind is excellent in reasoning, analysis and comparison, but it has its limits. Unless we train the mind to go beyond black and white thinking we are trapped in endless conflicts and wars. The dualistic mind causes conflicts in communities, families and couples, and separates us from ourselves. As a simple exercise, the next time someone disagrees with you, tell them you're glad they see differently and ask them to explain to you why they see differently. Listen and say to them, thank you for sharing. It shows that your understanding of the truth is universal.

It is also important to know that our level of consciousness affects our behavior and our relationship with others. Ken Wilber's classification of four levels of consciousness can also be applied to our perception of the truth.

4.1. Egocentrism

Egocentric people tend to see the truth from only their own perspective. Their reality is very narrow, and they think that they are their opinion. They have a natural inclination to reject another perspective when it does not fit their worldview. They do not separate others from their opinions. There is only one truth, and it is their truth. There is only one way, and it is their way. Egocentric people always want to be right and prove others wrong.

It is like the child's psyche. However, it is strange to see an adult acting like a child. This means something did not go well in the process of their growth and development. Leaders at the egocentric stage can easily become dictators. They treat those who disagree with them as adversaries, and sometimes like enemies. They want to get rid of them. An egocentric leader thinks that without them everything collapses. They have "the messiah complex," which means they are the only one everyone should listen to and praise. They can be controlling, make poor decisions, and blame others for their mistakes. Egocentric leaders do not know what it means to negotiate peace. There is only one way, which is their way, or they use violence.

Some people stay at this level and others take it to the next level when they face challenges that turn their inner world upside down. It is also possible that a coach or mentor will help them evolve to a higher level of consciousness.

4.2. Ethnocentrism

At the ethnocentric level, our interpretation of the truth centers on our ethnic group, religion or culture. Ethnocentric people see their group identity as superior to others. They consider rituals and traditions more important than principles. Their interaction with others is biased, although they are not aware of this. They always have a hidden agenda to change others to be like them, because diversity is threat for them.

The ethnocentric view of reality is highly exclusive. Those who do not see like them must change and become like them, or be excluded from their group. Tribalism characterizes this stage. They tend to protect their territory and fight anyone who appears to be a threat. There is only inclusion if you convert and start acting like them and think like them. Their religion is the only true one and everyone should join their religion, otherwise they will go to hell. Ethnocentrism can be extended into extreme nationalism, racism and xenophobia. Ethnocentric leaders can easily divide their group, organization or nation because they need to fight an enemy. Racial division, religious intolerance and ethnic wars are generally led by ethnocentric leaders.

The egocentric and ethnocentric levels are low levels of consciousness. No one should be content at those levels. We must seek a higher level.

4.3. Worldcentrism

At the worldcentric level, it all depends on the political ideology or the form of government that can spread to the rest of the world. Should the whole world become democratic or communist? People who are worldcentered have this program and it is carried by powerful nations like the USA, China, Russia, France and others. What economic system can spread to the rest of the world? Should it be capitalism or socialism? The World Bank and the International Monetary Fund are essentially instruments to support capitalism around the world. Their hidden agenda is to impose democracy as the ideal and unique form of government on the rest of the world.

The African system of government before colonialism was the monarchy, and this was rejected and condemned because it did not work in Europe. This state of mind is considered to be throwing out the baby with the bathwater. The problem is not the monarchy but the immature, irresponsible and greedy monarchs. Therefore, a good monarch will certainly do better than an immature and selfish leader in a democratic system. The world would not necessarily become a better world because we impose a system of governance on everyone. It is up to each country to choose its form of governance and to align itself with the principles of transformation, truth, love, restoration and choice.

However, it is much better to have worldcentric leaders than egocentric and ethnocentric leaders. Most of them are genuinely seeking a better world for all people. They are concerned about issues such as poverty across the world. Certain kinds of disease have been eradicated in developing countries because of worldcentric leaders.

4.4. Cosmocentrism

This highest level of consciousness is cosmocentric. People who are at this level transcend their ego. They have a universal vision of the cosmos which focuses not only on humanity but also on animals and nature. People at this stage tend to include everything, embrace and transcend everything. They really help improve other people's lives without expecting much from the world. In the modern era,

Martin Luther King Jr., Mahatma Gandhi, Mother Teresa, and many others have lived exemplary lives that fit the cosmocentric level. An example who certainly moved many in the world was Saint Francis of Assisi. We remember his famous quote: "Lord, make me an instrument of your peace. Where there is hatred, allow me to sow love."

We must not make the mistake of wanting to own the truth. We can only describe the truth from a point of view and never reach that which is absolute and universal in nature. We can only go there. The biggest problem we face when human beings want to understand the truth is that we take our perception as the universal truth. When we practice principles, we experience the truth. We can talk about transformation, but unless we are going through transformation, we don't yet know the truth. When we experience the ultimate reality, we are transformed from it and we are free from fear and arrogance. We no longer fight or run away when someone disagrees or sees differently.

We are mainly oriented towards knowledge not wisdom. Some people can be intellectually bright, but also unwise. You know they are not wise when they destroy their meaningful relationships just because they want to be right and prove others wrong. Wise people understand that they can't always be right, so they do their best to be in a good relationship. Wise people no longer jump into quick judgments and label and categorize people. They know that what they see is not always the full picture. They know they are showing the moon with their finger and their finger is not the moon, and they also leave room for the hidden part of the moon, which is the mystery.

We will never end the conflict in our families, in our communities and in our nations when we dwell in black and white thinking, good and bad perspectives, or we get rid of those who do not see things as we do.

5. Personal or experiential truth

Personal truths are experiences that confirm or disprove our beliefs. It should also be understood that this is a partial truth. Believing that God is love and experiencing that love are two different things. Personal truth is found in experience and not in opinions. Opinions come from what we have been taught to be true, as well as from our past experiences. Sometime one can have painful past experiences and they can become a filter that we use in describing reality.

It is said that, "Before the truth sets you free, it tends to make you miserable." Understanding one's own personal truth can be uncomfortable, especially when something you are not proud of is about to be revealed. Whenever you get too defensive and try to justify your argument, your shadow, your dark side comes to light. However, if you can be humble and patient enough, you will experience a personal transformation. Overreacting to things that make you uncomfortable is a clear sign that you have to face something within you that you are not proud of. There is a hidden truth that needs to be uncovered.

Think about it for a moment and ask yourself, why does this make me so uncomfortable? Instead of being reactive, reflect. This is how you uncover your truth. In the process, you must allow the false self, or the relative self, to be exposed, in order to lose its power. Then you can be in touch with the inner self. So, anytime you feel sad, angry, frustrated or disappointed, it has more to do with your shadow than what is happening outside of yourself. The best attitude is to be introspective, and, if you cannot handle it, talk to a mentor or coach or friend you trust. This approach is known as shadow boxing. Remember, shadow boxing can take a lifetime.

The problem with society is that it encourages people to look good, but not necessarily to be good. To be good you need to be genuine and speak with integrity. However, society tends not to value people who are truthful. You can speak clearly, use swear words, and obey all grammatical rules with their exceptions, and then you are seen as a good person. This is what gives us social status. Then we build a false sense of identity, superiority around title, position, intellectual knowledge, just to impress others and we hide behind our bad character. Many religious and political leaders pretend to be good while playing a game behind the scenes. If you easily believe in them, in what they call the truth, you can be lost. You can end up being exploited and lied to.

If we do not understand that knowing the truth is first to be humble, we cannot be free. When we are humble, we are also free to be honest and sincere. When we live with integrity, honesty and sincerity, we are living the truth and it will set us free. The biggest lesson to learn about the truth is to make sure that you are calm, humble, and patient when you are wrong about a problem. Make sure you learn from it. When what you believe to be true suddenly comes apart, you have to stay calm and thoughtful. When you have chosen humility, even in the midst of confusion of mind, you will experience true freedom. This is where your power is.

In conclusion, when describing the truth, you should use words such as "I believe," "I think, "my point of view is." When expressing your personal or relative truth, be authentic, responsible without blaming others. For example: "I feel judged," "I feel angry," "I am sad," "I struggle to love you," "I apologize for the misunderstanding," "I wonder why I can't see it as you see it," "I'm scared," "I'm confused." One of the best lessons in humility you can teach others is to tell them "you don't know!!!" It is always wise to put together knowing and not knowing. It is the path of wisdom.

6. The practice of listening

Listening is an effective way to discover personal truth. It is a skill to be learned. Most people want to talk, and the tendency is for people to listen in order to reply instead of listening to understand. Below are some steps you can take to find out the truth. This practice can extend into your professional life, especially when there is disagreement about a given topic. Knowing how to listen can also diffuse anger and resolve conflicts between people.

1. Listen without interrupting

2. Paraphrase what you hear

3. Ask clarifying questions

4. Observe body language (crossed arms, furrowed eyebrows, etc.)

5. Clarify the emotions that are expressed (anger, frustration, doubt, joy, inspiration, sadness)

6. Be present (not in the past or in the future)

7. Mental or intellectual dimension

The principle of truth is linked to the intellectual dimension. What do you feed your mind with? Reading and writing are exercises that develop the mind. Make the effort to read at least one book per month in your area of interest. Think about your vision in detail. Take on the challenge of reading one book per month. Take the time to write down your ideas and post them for the benefit of others. Remember, "who reads, leads." Ignorance is not an excuse. It is often said, "If you want to hide something from Africans, put it in a book." The African tradition values oral communication rather than written communication. However, reading and writing are essential to express your thoughts and ideas. It is also important that you teach others what you know. In fact, who teaches once learns twice.

We need constant training in the intellectual dimension, especially in our field of interest. Therefore, seminars and workshops are essential for constant intellectual growth. If possible, get the highest degree in your field and start teaching others. Moreover, writing a book can be difficult, but also rewarding intellectual work. Writing books and articles can give you references in your areas of passion. Make sure you know what you are talking about in order to gain the trust of others.

8. Case study

Once, I was teaching the principle of truth to a manager of a company and his team. I presented this image and asked everyone what they saw on the screen. Some said it was an old woman and others a young lady.

The manager insisted that the image was a young lady. He refuted the fact that it was an old woman. A member of his team said to him: "Manager, I am wondering why you are seeing a young lady, I see an old woman." The manager felt offended and insisted that he was right.

I tried to explain to the manager that he was right, but others weren't wrong about their description of the image. The manager became defensive and his voice became louder. He said: "It can't be an old woman; you guys are wrong." As we concluded the seminar, the atmosphere became tense.

Explain the reasons why the manager thought he was right and others were wrong.

How did he violate the principle of truth?

What lessons as a leader or manager did you learn from this story?

III. The Principle of Love

1. Definition

According to the *Merriam-Webster Dictionary*, love is a strong affection for another arising out of kinship or personal ties, such as maternal love for a child. It is also considered an attraction based on sexual desire, an affection based on admiration, benevolence or common interests. Love is also an assurance of affection, warm attachment, enthusiasm, unselfish loyal and benevolent concern for the good of another, such as the fatherly concern of God for humankind, brotherly concern for others, and a personal adoration of God.

Romantic love has always been a complex matter to discuss. Is romantic love real love? How does romantic love differ from the principle of love?

1.1. Romantic love

In his 1956 book *The Art of Loving*, psychologist Erich Fromm challenged the notion that love is a phenomenon which occurs without our control. Fromm believed it is a common mistake to confuse the intense feelings we experience when we fall in love at the beginning of a relationship with real love. The passionate and obsessive period that we dream of so much, due to all its excitement, can be part of a romantic relationship but not of love itself - it is only a phase and it will not last long.

Studies in neuroscience have confirmed Fromm's theory by clearly differentiating the early phase when we "fall in love" from the period of long-term commitment by detecting distinct activities in our blood and brain. Researchers have studied people who have just fallen in love and those who are in a long-term relationship. One observation shows the pattern of blood levels changing over time. Magnetic Resonance Imaging (MRI) studies of the brain support these results, showing activities in separate brain areas during each phase.

The phase where we "fall in love" invariably ends after 2 to 4 years; it's just the natural way a relationship begins. If we reduce love to the moment of romantic feeling alone, we will inevitably be disappointed. That is why there is a peak in relationship breakdowns after 2-4 years. In contrast, love is a lasting commitment which requires our active involvement at every step of the relationship. The principle of love is much deeper than a feeling.

Unfortunately, since the 18th century, romantic love was propagated as being true love and later the media (Hollywood, romance novels and fairy tales) supported the idea. Most people make choices based on their feelings, expecting that it will bring happiness. However, we omit the pain and the struggle part about real love. So, when people realize that there is no love without pain and some emotional bleeding and they were not prepared for the challenges, then they give up.

The basic reason why a romantic relationship starts out well and slowly deteriorates into hatred and resentment is because people seek to be loved but are not prepared to truly love. Are you able to say: *I trust myself; I am vulnerable enough to say how I feel; I am not afraid to lose my ego; I am in control of my negative emotions; I can be authentic and humble enough when I am challenged; I can forgive the unforgivable and ask for forgiveness with sincerity? I won't give up when things become hard?* That is the principle of love.

When we really love someone, someone other than ourself, our ego dies. The ego manifests itself in the superiority complex, protective and defensive behavior, and an attitude of blame. When you have realized that you are just a drop in the ocean and not the ocean itself, you can only be humble. Your life has meaning only when it serves a larger purpose. It is almost impossible to love someone if you are afraid of losing yourself. There is no love when fear, insecurity and past hurts guide your life. We don't get married to be happy; we get married to grow. When we the pay the price to grow in love eventually we mature, and mature people are happy people. Marriage is a win-win relationship. A win-lose or lose-win will, in the long-term, conclude in a lose-lose situation.

As an example, during my first three years of marriage I had a lot of problems. I suffered a lot because as an intellectual I like intellectual discussions. I was well trained to be right instead of truly loving. I liked to argue and be defensive about stupid things. Winning in a discussion only nourishes the ego; it does not deepen your love for others. We don't get married to be right, but to love.

There are three factors that determine romantic love. These are beauty, sexuality and emotional transfer.

1.2. Physical beauty

Physical beauty is like a mirage. It seems real from a distance, but the closer you get, the more you realize it's not real. Seeking love based on physical beauty can result in great disappointment. The mirage is also chasing after material things as a source of happiness. Inner beauty is the expression of the soul and spiritual qualities. It takes maturity to understand that not everything that shines is gold. What is seen is not always what it is. We have to differentiate authenticity from appearance.

1.3. Sexuality

Most people confuse sex and love. Love can be expressed though sex but sex in itself is not necessary an act of love. Believing that sex is love can be a trap that leads to sexual addiction and all its negative implications, such as abuse, rape, emotional violence, sexual diseases, unwanted children, and so forth.

Porn movies are dangerous for the mind. They are the number one killer of marriage. Porn is completely an illusion. It creates the expectation that the partner can perform sexual acts like in the porn video, which is completely impossible. In real life, it does not work, and it can lead to serious disappointment in a relationship.

I once asked some couples in their 70s and 80s about how important sex was in their life. Their response was always the same: "We care more about intimacy than sex itself."

1.4. Emotional transference

During our childhood we naturally get attached to those who share our deepest concerns and aspirations: parents, siblings, close friends, etc. As life goes by, we lose those relationships. Parents die, siblings and friends move away or die. When we become adults, we recall those meaningful relationships from the subconscious mind and project them onto new people and that triggers those past emotional needs. This generates an energy called romance, falling in love, or "coup de foudre." We pursue those relationships until we realize they are not the person we were projecting, and then we can be very disappointed and withdraw. Emotional transference can also be a negative experience that we had in our past life and projected into a new person. This is the reason we do not know why we cannot get along with certain people we just met, or feel suddenly attracted to someone we just met.

Physical beauty, sex and emotional transfer do not last long. Therefore, it is recommended not to make lifelong decisions based on them.

2. Real love

Real love is primarily a principle, not just a mere feeling. It is act of "giving," sacrificing and committing to someone, an idea or a project. However, in the process of sacrificing there is always pain involved. There is no relationship where people don't gets hurt from time to time. Unfortunately, many people do not know what to do with pain. They withdraw, pretend or attack. A relationship where partners do not know what to do with pain will sooner or later be a failure.

We all need someone in our life who gets that basic point about relationships. Someone who understands that when it gets hurtful there is a healthy way of processing it. Someone who knows how to deal with the dark side of the soul and come out from it. Knowing that pain will be part of the game, and learning to process pain through sincere self-reflection, is the way to a stronger, healthier and long-term relationship.

It does not matter how great you think you are. This is a principle everyone needs to understand and practice to see personal and professional growth. It does not mean you have to be successful all the time, but it is a sincere commitment to grow in love. Love isn't always fun; it is a whole package of fun and pain. It doesn't matter how compatible you are, how often you make each other smile, how committed you are. You will face tough times in the relationship. There are moments when you will fail to understand each other and you will drive each other crazy. As the scripture says, there is a time to hate and a time to love. The more you are intimate, the more likely you will step on each other's toes, so be ready for the tough journey of love. Remember the wedding ceremony is not marriage itself: Wedding is a day and marriage lasts forever.

That is why, before making the choice to marry someone, make sure you are deciding that you will not easily reconsider no matter what happens in the process. This is a journey to grow stronger, wiser, and mature as a couple. The great lover has two hearts: One bleeds and the other endures. So, when you chose to love then you will suffer. In fact, those you love may neglect your love, brush it away, reject you, and might not care much. When you are internally peaceful and secure then you can afford to keep giving.

This kind of love has a higher purpose. Let's say you want to win your boss's heart so that he can trust you. The process to win someone else's trust can be very difficult. But if you are willing to pay the price, because you care about the vision and the mission of the company, it is okay to suffer and endure the process. If it is your own business and you want to win the trust of your customers, you keep investing in them. Remember the goal of suffering and enduring is higher than the people who are involved. It must have something to do with your life's purpose, a legacy you would like to live behind. In that case you can afford to be patient and keep giving and investing.

You choose to get married because you want to mature in love, and the process of maturation is difficult and painful. When you stop loving, you stop growing. Those who refuse to grow will suffer on their journey. They will dwell in resentment, blame and accusation. Those who chose to grow will also suffer, but they will enjoy the peace of maturity later. The same principle is applicable in business. If you give up on your dream because the process is painful you might regret it. If you do not give up you will certainly suffer, but you will reap the fruit of your efforts.

3. Building trust through love

Most people make promises easily and do not come through. Every promise we make creates an anticipation in someone else's mind. When we do not fulfill our promises, people can be seriously disappointed. Therefore, before making promises, make sure you will follow through. Unfulfilled promises negatively impact the level of trust. If you want to improve and sustain the level of trust between you and your loved one, your partner, then make sure you do what you say. Do not promise what you cannot do; or promise with a window of uncertainty. You could say, "I would like to buy you a dress, but I am not sure yet. If things go well financially, I will try my best." In this case, you are telling the other person that it might not happen. You can make a greater impact when you surprise that person.

Unfulfilled promises destroy your credibility. You might break promises sometimes, but it should never become a habit. Remember you cannot love someone you do not trust. Build trust or rebuild trust with your promises, even the small ones. If you do not keep your promises, people might resent you for that because they will feel betrayed. If you tell your team, let's meet for a conference on Monday at 10am, then make it happen. If you promise your customers a product, do it and stop making excuses. This sounds simple, but it is one of the most important factors for success in relationships and business.

On the other side, not everyone understands this basic point. Therefore, you cannot expect much from others. When people promise something, hope for it but do not keep a high expectation. If the person fulfills their promise, enjoy that moment and thank them for keeping their promise. However, if they fail, don't make a big deal out of it; just move on with your life.

Hope is not expectation. Expectation creates disappointment and frustration while hope is giving many chances to a person to better themselves. Encourage others to keep their promises without being mad at them. Try to be patient as much as you can and keep teaching by your actions. Do not get mad and start blaming someone because they failed you. Give others another chance to make it right.

4. Love in the family

Mother Teresa famously said that if you want to make this world a better place, "go home and love your family." It all starts at home. To understand your adult life, you need to revisit your upbringing. Why do most people seek first to be loved? Growing up, most people received not enough love or conditional love from their parents. "Unless you do this, you will not get my love. If you make a mistake you get punished." That is called conditional love. When we reach adulthood, our cup is empty of unconditional love and we are still seeking someone to fill up that cup. This is called expectation.

Love is not an expectation. We are literally incapable of giving love unconditionally. We are emotionally set to receive love from our partner first. We unconsciously seek someone to meet all our emotional needs. That is why we end up disappointed, frustrated and angry. We think that our partner causes our disappointment, but in fact it is rooted in the fact that we did not experience love unconditionally before meeting him. So, because our partner has not experienced it himself, it impossible for him to give it. Both expecting from each other, and not getting what they want, leads to them getting stuck and distancing from each other.

It is like someone who is drowning and seeking help who grasps the nearest person, which happens to be you. Unfortunately, if you are not a good swimmer, both of you will start to drown. You will certainly hate him for putting your life in danger. However, he was not trying to harm you; he was trying to save himself. Has not intentionally trying to harm you, he was desperately seeking help. Someone who is a good swimmer could have saved him. It is the same thing with the principle of love. Unless you experienced it, you cannot give it, and you might blame your partner for not giving it to you while, in fact, he himself does not have it to give.

You need someone who already experienced it and can help you: a coach, a mentor, a wise friend who will first truly love you even when you make mistakes; someone you can be honest with about your faults and he will still accept you for who you are. Then, you can gradually learn to give back until it becomes a habit. In fact, it is a big mistake to believe that your partner will fulfill all your emotional needs in a relationship.

Love is also seeking to understand the other first. Unfortunately, most people put themselves first and do not even try to understand others. That is called "fish love." We love the fish because it tastes good, not because we care about it. We just care about how it will fulfill our needs. So, we kill it and eat it, and feel satisfied with the taste. Real love requires that you think about the happiness of the other person first, and vice versa. When both partners are seeking to understand first, then a dynamic of love is generated for the joy and happiness of both partners. This kind of love is applicable in other relationships, such us friendships, family, coworkers, etc.

Parenthood is crucial for the future of the children. In fact, emotionally absent parents will raise children who feel insecure. Children need to feel that their parents are present, especially when they go through the challenges of life. It is important for the formation stage of a child. Abusive and violent parents tend to raise children who will accept violence done to others or themselves as normal. When they get into a relationship and are challenged, violence becomes the way to solve issues they face. Immature and irresponsible parents tend to raise children who never want to take responsibility for their wrongdoings. If you smoke, you can't teach your kids not to smoke, because children are seeking models not lecturers. It's not what you tell the kids that helps them be successful in life, but what kind of model you are for them.

You cannot give what you have not received. If you have tea in a glass and I ask you for coffee, I will not receive coffee but tea. Don't expect others to give you what they never received themselves. If you did not receive real love from your parents, it will be difficult to give it when you become an adult. Therefore, find a father or mother figure.

5. Choosing your future spouse

The choice of your future spouse will shape your destiny. Therefore, do not rush to get married because you are feeling lonely or want to feel secure. Do not get married because your best friend got married. Do not get married because you need financial support. It is a lifetime decision. Remember this is your personal decision for a long-term commitment, not your pastor's, your imam's, your parents' or friends'. You can involve others in the decision-making process, ask them for advice, but never feel compel to choose because of others.

How do you know it is the right decision you are making? Be patient and observe. Do not just rely on your feelings alone. Take time to know who you are getting involved with. Do not rush such a decision to have sex and marry someone because you are feeling attracted to her or him. To increase the chances of success for the relationship, you want to start with a strong foundation. Explore your deeper motivation: Why are you getting involved with that person? Look into your visions, your goals, your cultures, and discuss with them the pros and cons. Discuss your future, your financials, and come to a win-win agreement.

If there is red flag do not proceed even if you are having strong feelings for that person. It is not because you have strong feelings for them that he or she is the one. He is the right person because you are committed to one another to grow together for the rest of your lives. The question is, can I still be with this person even if I do not have feelings for him anymore? What is it about him in terms of internal quality that will sustain a relationship? Do we have a common or shared vision? Are we committed beyond the feeling of the moment? If the answers are yes, then move forward with the relationship. The chances of success are high. If not, you had better wait until you get some clarity.

After getting into a relationship, you must understand the dynamics of love between man and woman. In general, a man feels loved when he is respected and served by his partner. As a woman, try your best not to disrespect your man, especially in public. When a man feels disrespected, his dignity is trampled, and that is how you will lose him. If you want a successful relationship, as a woman, keep serving and respecting your spouse unconditionally. On the other side, a woman feels loved when a man chooses to die for her, not literally of course! It means to sacrifice time and money and to defend and protect her no matter what. A woman will feel secure, safe and emotionally connected, when the man truly sacrifices for her. That is why the Bible says: "Husbands love your wives as Christ loved the church; he died for the church. ... Wives respect and serve your husbands as the church served and respects the Christ."

This is the dynamic of the relationship between man and woman. It is the foundation for growth for both the husband and the wife. Remember, no rituals or special blessing from whoever, no gigantic wedding, special prayers in churches, in mosques, in synagogues or in temple will guarantee the success of your marriage. No special prayer from the bishop, the imam, or the rabbi will guarantee a successful marriage.

Real love is the cement that makes a successful marriage. In fact, growth is part of the journey and there will be no peace in the relationship without a sincere commitment to growth. Remember, refusing to grow, especially in marriage, is a violation of the principle of love and it will lead to separation or divorce. The common vision is to become one in love, even if we have different characters. The process is difficult, so it is important to learn the basic skills to resolve couple conflicts so that we do not carry past wounds and resentment. Have sex as much as you can. A good sex life deepens the bonds and connection between couples. It also reduces stress. A healthy relationship creates a safer environment for children to grow. The children become emotionally stable and are better leaders in life.

To end this point, I invite you to mediate on these words from the Bible, 1 Corinthians 13:4-8:

> Love is patient, love is kind. It does not envy, it does not boast, it is not proud. It does not dishonor others, it is not self-seeking, it is not easily angered,

it keeps no record of wrongs. Love does not delight in evil but rejoices with the truth. It always protects, always trusts, always hopes, and always perseveres. Love never fails. But where there are prophecies, they will cease; where there are tongues, they will be stilled; where there is knowledge, it will pass away.

For those who are Muslims, remember that the Qur'an contains 114 chapters and 113 of them start with the term, "In the name of Allah, the most merciful and the most gracious." The only chapter in the entire Qur'an that does not begin this way is the chapter on repentance. The Islamic holy book is telling us that we must sincerely repent, which basically means humble ourselves because we receive mercy and grace from God all our lives.

Grace means you get what you do not deserve. The love of God is given to us for free. We do not need to work hard to get it. Therefore, we should give to others without condition. Mercy is when you do not get what you deserve. We make mistakes and we deserve to be punished on many occasions, but we don't always get punished by God. We experience grace and mercy throughout our lives, and we should also express grace and mercy towards other people around us.

Fear is the absence of love. The energy of love is already present in the universe and accessible to all. We just need to learn how to tap into that reality. We access love by being present with God.

6. Emotional dimension

The principle of love is directly linked to the emotional dimension.

Where is your heart? Are you emotionally connected to your vision? If not, let it go and seek something you feel connected to. People will challenge your character. Life will challenge you with failures. People will oppose you, discourage you, betray you. But if you heart is connected to your vision you must keep going. Those who give up are those who failed. They failed because their heart was never truly connected to that vision or they fear the painful process. If you give up, it means you NEVER wanted it in the first place. So, make sure you want it and you truly mean it before you jump in the boat to pursue a specific dream. If someone tells you it is impossible, prove to them that it is possible. If they want to get in your way to stop you pursuing your dream, leave them and move on. No one and nothing can stop you achieving your dream except yourself. If you love it, you will get it.

Real love and emotional growth are connected: We grow emotionally through sacrifice, self-giving, and constant engagement in a relationship. Emotional intelligence is an essential factor for success in our relationships. We become what we like. Do you have trouble loving others? Find a mentor with whom you can experience real love. Regarding your calling, ask yourself: What do I love so that I can give my life for it? If there is no answer, reflect and pray about it. Love is giving time and energy, including the struggles that go with it. The process of loving is painful, but the outcome of real love is inner peace and happiness.

When love is broken, we need restoration. In the process of building a strong relationship hurt and brokenness can happen, so we need the principle of restoration to get back on track.

7. Case study

Aicha and Hamed met in college in the Law Department. Hamed was a young and brilliant student. He was praised by many professors. One day, Aicha asked Hamed if it was okay to study with him. She needed help. At first, Hamed felt uncomfortable but he accepted Aicha's request. Aicha was very beautiful. A devoted Muslim, she always performed her daily prayers with sincerity, and wore her "Hijab" (veil) whenever she was in public. A few weeks later, Hamed and Aicha became very close friends. They started spending more time together. There was no doubt that they loved each other. They decided to make the relationship official, despite some resistance from Aicha's parents. The parents wanted Aicha to finish her studies first. A few months later, they got married and were very happy together.

For the first 5 years, everything was going well for them. They had 2 daughters and Aicha was expecting another child. Hamed had become a prominent lawyer. Aicha, unfortunately, could not continue her studies due to family circumstances. She stayed home to take care of the children. As time went by, Hamed's behavior start to change and Aicha did not know why. He would come home late and sometimes spent the night at work. Arguments and fights happened constantly over little things. Hamed would get angry and ignore her for days.

One day, Aicha checked Hamed's phone and found pictures and messages with another woman. She was shocked and speechless. She discovered that the man she loved was having an affair with another woman. She later confronted him with the evidence. Hamed could not deny the facts. He confessed that for 3 years he had been in love with one of his lawyer colleagues. They had a child, and she was currently pregnant. Aicha's world turned upside down. She cried for hours. She felt betrayed and was not sure what to do. Hamed told her that he no longer loved her, but he still wanted to keep the relationship for the sake of the kids.

1. Do you think Aicha and Hamed really loved each other? Explain?

2. If you were Aicha, what would you do?

3. If you were Hamed, what would you do?

4. What are some of the factors that contributed to the failure of the relationship?

IV. The Principle of Restoration

1. Definition

According to the *Merriam-Webster Dictionary*, restoration is an act of restoring, or the condition of being restored, such as bringing back to a former position or condition. It is a reinstatement or the restoration of peace. It is a restitution or repairing to an unimpaired or improved condition. Restoration is also a representation or reconstruction of the original form.

2. Principle of restoration

In reality, no relationship can return to its exact original state. It takes on a new form, a new dynamic, a new breath. Restoration has two essential components: The first is forgiveness and the second is reparation, reconstruction or reconciliation. Many people confuse the two components. Forgiveness comes first and reconciliation or reparation second. You cannot reconcile unless you forgive first.

Forgiveness is about releasing the pain from an emotional hurt. It is not directed towards the other. It is a personal exercise to regain your emotional well-being. If you don't forgive, you become a prisoner of resentment and this can negatively impact your emotional and sometimes physical health. As Nelson Mandela says, "Resentment is drinking poison and hoping the other dies."

Reconciliation is a process of renewing a broken relationship. This means the parties in conflict have a clear idea of the outcome of the relationship. This implies an integrated negotiation and agreement acceptable to the conflicting parties. Sandrine Lefranc, researcher in social sciences at the Université Paris-Sorbonne Sciences Po Paris, defines reconciliation in these terms: "In its form of public, governmental action, most often, reconciliation is supposed to reorganize the relationship of society to its violent past by bringing it back to an earlier state of supposed national unity."

On an individual level, depending on the importance of the person in your life, or the project you have in common, you can choose to be reconciled or not. In all human relationships, there is a risk to hurt one another. This is why we must learn to forgive every day. Who has never been hurt? We have all been hurt a few times. Therefore, we must learn to let go of grudges and resentment again and again.

3. Managing emotions

The word emotion comes from the Latin word "emotus" which means "disturb," and so is not to be confused with the love, peace, joy and tranquility which are the fruits of the spirit. Emotions such as anger, frustration, sadness, jealousy, fear, discouragement, disappointment and guilt are experiences we all go through. The problem is not the emotion itself, but when the emotion controls our actions.

Human beings in general react in two ways whenever they get hurt or threatened: either they attack or they withdraw from the relationship. Knowing how to manage your emotions is learning not to react negatively when you get hurt or threatened. Breaking up a relationship when you are hurt is a form of punishment for the other. It is unconsciously telling that person that they no longer deserve your love.

Defensive behavior, blame, attacks, verbal and physical abuse are the surest way to fail in personal life and in business. These are the causes of divorce, separation between business partners, communities, organizations, families and so on. They can also lead to violent wars and destructions. When we are hurt, we put ourselves in the position of victims, we blame the other and then we judge, condemn, we even kill, expecting to heal from our pain.

Actually, overreacting when we are hurt does not help us grow, it negatively affects others, and it does not help us either. This is why we must learn a third way in order to better manage our emotions.

4. The third way

The third way is not attacking or withdrawing from a relationship when you are hurt. It involves an introspection in order to begin the process of personal or collective healing. Leaders capable of introspection in challenging times can heal themselves and others involved in the painful situation. This principle of restoration, when it is practiced well, transforms in a healthier way both personal and professional life.

Leaders incapable of letting go of and processing their emotions are a real danger for their communities. It is like a blind man leading other blind men into a ditch: Sooner or later they will fail tragically together.

Since our childhood, poorly handled emotional wounds have remained latent in our subconscious. Whenever we face a new crisis situation, it awakens the wounds of the past and therefore our reaction is spontaneous. The underlying reason for our anger is not the other; someone just triggers "old demons" in us. This person is a mirror for our subconscious. For example, if you feel always abandoned by others and this makes you very sad, you will have to revisit your childhood and see how it relates to sadness. Do not blame someone around you, because an emotionally absent parent can be the cause of such a recurrent feeling in adulthood.

Emotions are the response of the body to our thoughts. If your thoughts are mostly negative, your reactions will be negative. It is a biological phenomenon. Your thoughts are the teachings of others and the experiences of the past. A young girl who has suffered from her parents' divorce will tend to be afraid of marriage, thinking that the same phenomenon will happen again. Behind thoughts is the subconscious, where information and experiences from the past are stored. It is the subconscious in most cases that directs our reactions.

Carrying our negative thoughts can even cause depression and serious mental illness.

Whenever a negative thought comes to your mind, remember that this thought is passing through. Do not feed it; let it go because it does not belong to you. You can also weaken it with positive thinking or positive action. For example, if someone insults you and you feel hurt, instead of reacting violently, try to stay calm and think positively, "This person is certainly going through difficult times and needs help instead." You will see that the wound will gradually lose its power and you will be free again.

In reality, when you are mature, nothing can offend you to the point where you lose control completely. The key to your success in your endeavors is to develop self-control and gain the ability to manage your emotions. People will hurt you consciously or unconsciously anyway. You have to learn to forgive over and over again throughout your life. Life itself will not always give you gifts. There are times when life disciplines you with great severity, such as illnesses, accidents, and even the loss of a loved one. You have to learn to forgive life itself.

5. Victimization

Victimization consists of putting oneself in the position of one who suffers the wrong and asking for justice. When we are hurt, we put ourselves in the position of victim, and this can also lead to wanting revenge. As long as the other has to equally and absolutely pay for what they have done to us, the infernal cycle of violence will not end. Sometimes it is better to let go when that contributes to ending the cycle of violence. Leaders know how to lose so that the both parties can have peace in their relationship. This is not an easy path to take and people can exploit it as weakness. However, when we have the courage to forgive others and move out of victimhood, we can be free again. We can also see a new opportunity life is offering to us.

For example, many Africans keep blaming Europe for colonization, imperialism and slavery, which caused poverty and suffering in Africa for centuries. Those who do this put themselves in the position of eternal victims. It is true that colonization brought a lot problems to the African continent. However, it is time to take responsibility. Blame will not solve the real problem and Africa will not stop experiencing political instability and poverty.

Albert Einstein said that within every problem lies a great opportunity. Behind an injustice hides a hidden mission and sometimes even a blessing. An American saying puts it well: "If life gives you lemons, make lemonade out of them and sell it to those in need." Great people have made a difference, understanding that they can respond differently to the injustice they face in life. Those such as Mandela, Gandhi, Martin Luther King Jr., Jesus, Mother Teresa, Prophet

Muhammad, Rev. Moon, Malcom X, and many others have shown that injustice is also an opportunity for growth and success.

For example, Nelson Mandela, after spending 27 years in prison and finally being released and working his way to become the first black president in south Africa, decided that the victims and the perpetrators must discuss what happened and move on. The famous dialogue, Truth and Reconciliation, became a model on the national level that laid a foundation for a new South African state to be built after all that violent conflict.

One story that I heard a while ago was that Nelson Mandela went to a restaurant with one of his friends for dinner. At dinner, a white man was sitting nearby watching them and looking scared. This man looked at Nelson Mandela from time to time, but you could tell he was not doing well. At one point, Nelson Mandela invited him to his table and asked the restaurant to serve this man food and drink. As he ate, the man's hand was shaking and he seemed preoccupied. Finally, Mandela took care of the bill and said goodbye to him, shaking his hand and told him he was glad to see him again.

As they left the area, Mandela's friend asked him who this guy was. He looked sick and strange. Mandela replied: "He is not sick; he is just afraid. This guy was my persecutor when I was in prison. I think he recognized me, and he's scared that I will take my revenge." Mandela said that this guy was so mean to him that when he was thirsty and asked for water to drink, he would beat him and piss on him. His friend asked him how he could still be nice to such an obnoxious person? Mandela had learned a great lesson in forgiveness, reminding everyone that:

> No one is born hating another person because of the color of his skin, or his background, or his religion. People must learn to hate, and if they can learn to hate, they can be taught to love, for love comes more naturally to the human heart than its opposite.

That is also the philosophy of Ubuntu that Nelson Mandela put forward as an African value: "I am, because you are" is the way forward for the African continent.

How can you teach others to forgive? You forgive them first. Forgiveness is not a mathematical concept that you can explain to someone. You practice forgiveness and what frees you frees others. This is the meaning of seeing the other side of the coin whenever we encounter injustice. Being able to see the other side of the coin, you don't waste your time on your enemies, but instead focus on the new opportunity that presents itself to you. Observe the surroundings, and you will certainly find a diamond where you have fallen.

6. Restorative justice

The aim of the judicial system is to discover the truth, to allow victim and perpetrator to tell their version of the truth, and apply what the law recommends. Unfortunately, this approach also has a negative outcome, which consist of a systematic condemnation of the perpetrator. Sometimes a mistake is done to innocent people who become a victim of injustice for a crime they have not committed. The judicial system is led by human beings and therefore it is not perfect. From a principled perspective, prison should be a place of education and raising people's consciousness, instead of making it a matter of punishment. When the perpetrator admits his wrong, a restorative approach to justice is much better that a punitive one.

The restorative justice process begins with the search for truth. This approach is not about proving others wrong and playing the victim, but telling the story of your pain, what you have been through, and how you are dealing with it currently. It is important for the perpetrator to hear the story, and it is also important for the him to tell his story. Listening to the truth from several angles, both parties end up understanding that everyone has their share of responsibility in a conflict.

Then the next process is to exercise humility by asking forgiveness for causing pain to others in order to facilitate emotional healing. This approach also requires the courage to forgive the other in order to create the conditions for a possible reconciliation. Finally, it is important to do some reparation of possible wrongs; that is justice. At the end of the day, the protagonists can choose to build a future together if they want to, but they don't have to. It is up to them to decide to reconcile and work together for a better future or not. In general, when the process of restorative justice is successful, chances are high for reconciliation.

Capital punishment is the most inhumane approach to punitive justice. We do not give the person who committed a crime a chance to repent and change to be a better person. Punitive justice creates fear and mistrust among us. Restorative justice is the hope and future of humanity. Many people come out of prison with resentful hearts and can end up doing worse than you might imagine. It is true that not everyone can repent of their mistakes, so those who do not repent deserve to be imprisoned and held accountable for their wrongdoing. Ultimately, inmates must be educated and supported to return to serve society.

Restoration is about helping the victim forgive by providing the necessary psychological support and materials as we seek the truth through the legal process. When the truth is known, who did what and why, the condemnation follows. When the culprit has admitted his mistake and has asked for forgiveness, reconciliation must be granted by amnesty.

The main goal of restorative justice is to restore broken relationships and promote peace and sustainable development. Punishment leads to revenge sooner or later. Political leaders, with the help of religious leaders and psychologists, should be involved in post-conflict peacebuilding. The process of rebuilding a nation must prioritize restorative justice in the name of lasting peace.

The use of force

There are occasions when the use of force becomes necessary to address a critical situation. The use of force to resolve human problems should never be the norm, but rather the exception. The use of force can help restore the balance of power in certain situations. For example, the use of the nuclear bomb to end World War II was a brutal action, but it helped to end the war. This is not the ideal, but sometimes it is necessary to end violence. Even nature gives us signs through tornadoes and earthquakes that there is a need for balance. As you can see, there are not earthquakes and tornadoes every day. Therefore, violence and the use of force must never be the norm in society either.

The use of force can help protect the most vulnerable in a situation of violence or open conflict. In such a case, it is important that a higher force intervenes in order to protect the vulnerable in a violent situation. In most cases, these are unarmed adults, children, women and elderly.

The use of force is also allowed in some situations of self-defense. If someone comes into your house and seeks to harm your family, your primary responsibility is to protect your family at the cost of your life. In this case it is a moral responsibility to protect your loved ones against a dangerous situation.

In other situations, such as social protest, it is important that anyone who wants to bring change through protest must use a non-violent approach. This requires that the protestors have self-control and a leader who is modeling it. In response to peaceful protestors, the use of force by the police is not always the best approach. The police must protect, or make sure things do not turn into violence. Unfortunately, in most cases things do not happen peacefully.

Normally, power must not be used for selfish ends. That is why to build or rebuild stable nations armed forces are trained to protect citizens. However, as long as there are immature people in society, mechanisms must be put in place to frame and guide human development. Violence may become necessary to counter violence, but only in exceptional cases.

In terms of moral responsibility on an international scale, this example is typical: When UN forces did not intervene in Rwanda, 800,000 innocent people lost their lives. The genocide could have been avoided by using a positive force. We often hear "No Justice No Peace" but we should actually say "No Peace No Justice."

The notion of fairness can be very complex, depending on the context. Life itself is not fair in many ways. One wonders why someone was born into a rich nation and has all it takes to be successful and others are born into a poor nation with hardly enough to survive. It seems unfair. So, if life itself is not fair, how can we expect imperfect human beings to be perfectly fair? The notion of justice is an ideal to which we all aspire. In fact, the notion of justice remains only an ideal as long as imperfect human beings are dealing with one another. This does not mean that we should not do our best to seek fairness for those who wrongly suffered, but we should also understand that the notion of justice is complex. Sometimes we can cause more injustice by trying to serve justice.

The best way to create a just society is to focus on merit, so that those who give their best will benefit from their effort. Additionally, each citizen is treated fairly. At the same time, it will also be necessary to take into account the fact that not all have the same human potential. Although we are all born equal, we are not all born healthy, we are not all born with a golden spoon in our mouth, we are not all born with the same character and gifts. Therefore, as Einstein said "Everyone is a genius. But if you judge a fish by its ability to climb a tree, it will live its whole life believing that it is stupid." This is why we must instead build an integrated, diverse and pluralistic society while respecting the principles of development.

The ideal of justice is to create conditions so that each citizen can live their passion while embracing the principle of growth and development. It is profoundly unfair to force someone to become a medical doctor when their deep desire is to become a soccer player. There is only one life, so everyone must fully live the life they are destined to with the guidance of mentors. The educational system should be reformed so that it empowers children to uncover their talents and gifts so that they live a meaningful life.

7. Grieving

Grief is the emotional and mental pain we experience when we lose a loved one. Loss is painful; it is hard to detach emotionally from someone or something we love. Grief is universal; therefore, it is part of human life. To better grieve and heal from emotional pain, it is important to understand that life is a natural cycle which consists of first attaching to others and then letting go at the appropriate time.

We are born and are drawn to life and we slowly attach ourselves to our parents, spouses, family members, money, the environment, work, ideas, title, material possessions, etc. At some point, life reminds us that we must learn to let go, and we let go in order to heal from emotional pain. That is why it is better to learn to accept that the time will come when we have to give it all up and go.

When I worked as a spiritual counselor in a hospital, I saw people dying. Some, even on their death bed, struggled over unfinished business because of some attachment to things they never wanted to let go of while they were living in this world. You can see the indescribable suffering they go through at the end of their physical life. I have seen some people die in peace, with tranquility, because they learned to detach themselves from this material world, which in fact is only an illusion. Attachment leads to unnecessary suffering; we have to let go of everything we think is important and die in peace. As the saying goes, "We are born naked and we will leave naked." It is not just about nudity in terms of clothing, but also in terms of possession and attachment to the material world. This also includes all the past wounds we could never let go of. It is crucial to learn to let go of the negative emotions of the past in order to be completely free from resentment.

I was once giving advice to a young woman who was very angry with her husband. He left her after many years of marriage. She constantly blamed him for making her miserable and angry. I asked her if she got angry before meeting her husband. If so, what was causing this anger? She paused and admitted that she got mad at people or things that didn't suit her. Then I told her that her anger was not caused by her husband, it was caused by her own fear of detachment.

We have to learn to accept that our happiness does not depend on those who leave us. Of course, we have to grieve and regain our emotional health. In fact, if you do not grieve correctly, you will pass it on to those around you. Life asks us to let come what comes and let go of what goes. This is the meaning of inner peace and inner happiness.

To better illustrate this point, here is a story that will certainly help you. There was a Buddhist monk who led an ascetic life and received food from people in his neighborhood. A family nearby decided to bring him food every day. They sent their teenage daughter to bring food to the monk, and he graciously received it and thanked the family for their kindness. One day, the parents realized that their teenage daughter was pregnant. They asked her who the father was, and she replied that it was the Buddhist monk. They got angry and went to the monk and insulted him, calling him names. He bowed his head and remained silent and did not response to the all the verbal attacks.

When the baby was born, the girl's parents took the baby to the monk. They told him he had to take responsibility for his actions. It was a way of punishing him. The monk again didn't say anything and took the baby and started to take care of him. A few months later, the young girl, feeling so much guilt for lying and with her conscience bothering her, decided to tell her parents the truth. It was not the monk who was responsible for her pregnancy but a young boy who was her boyfriend in the neighborhood. She was so afraid to confess this to her parents that she had lied to them.

The parents, angry and upset again, went and picked up the baby. They told the monk that he was not the baby's father, that they had made a mistake, and that they did not think the monk could take care of the baby. The monk replied, "I enjoyed my time with the baby. He was so cute and lovely. Now it's time for me to let go." The Buddhist monk understood that the root of all suffering is attachment. He didn't get attached to the idea that he was the baby's father and the baby belonged to him.

It is a lesson in life for most of us. We get attached to people, things, ideas, names, a way of life and we never want to give up on them. In fact, nothing belongs to us in this world: Even our own body does not belong to us. We do not own anything. We use things and relate with people, and we must learn to leave everything when the time comes.

8. Socio-emotional dimension

The principle of restoration is directly linked to the socio-emotional dimension of being. This is sometimes referred to as social intelligence. This principle is to see not only the evil in your enemies but also the opportunity that the enemy offers for you to grow. There will always be people who oppose you or the way you want to do things. They are unknowingly playing their role in the progress of your success. If they give you a hard time, forgive them and continue your mission. If they are important in your life, go ahead and reconcile with them, forgive them and continue your journey without any guilty conscience.

We are not here on a collective journey; we are here on an individual journey. Some people cross our path to help us learn lessons and others to help us grow. Some are also tremendous blessings. At the end of our life, we are taking our last breath alone.

Most people when faced with challenges automatically blame or accuse others, lose motivation and give up. That is called failure. It is recommended to keep building your social network, and life itself will put the right people in your life to help you achieve your dreams. You must also forgive not only people but also life itself, so that when you take your last breath you do so with a deeply peaceful heart.

9. Case study: Forgiveness

There was a lady called Sindhutai who was born in a poor village in India. She never had any education. As a little girl, she wanted to go to school but she could not afford it because her family was poor and she was asked to care of the buffaloes and cows. When she turned 9 years old, she was married to a man who was 30 older than her. By the time she turned 19, she had three sons and she was pregnant again.

In the village there was a man who was exploiting the people: He would make them work without giving them any money; he would force women to work hard without giving them practically anything. Everyone was afraid of him. One day Sindhutai told the local collector who was overseeing the place and the man was arrested by the police. A few days later he was released from jail and was furious when he found out it was Sindhutai who had reported him to the police. So, he went and told Sindhutai's husband a lie. He said you are such a fool; your wife is having sexual affairs with so many men. He went further and told him that the child that she was carrying now was not the husband's; he was the father of the child. He said, "I have been having sex with her also."

The husband got so angry that he went to Sindhutai and started accusing her of betrayal and cheating. The conversation became uncontrollable, and the husband became violent and kicked her several times in her stomach to kill her and the child she was carrying. She became unconscious and started bleeding and he thought she was dead. So he dragged her to the cowshed and believed that people would think that the cows killed her.

She was unconscious for a few hours. When she woke up later, she found one cow right there in front of her protecting her. The cow was keeping any dangerous animals away from her until she woke up. Even when the in-laws came to make sure she was dead, the cow chased them away with its horns. She regained consciousness and give birth to a baby girl under the cow's protection. She said she took a rock and cut her umbilical cord, taking her 20 slices to get free from it. For hours and hours, the cow protected Sindhutai. When she had gained enough strength, she embraced the cow and promised, "as you protected me when I was in great need, I will also protect others in need."

She had no place to go as no one would give her a home because of their traditions. Even her biological family repudiated her because of tradition: She was considered cursed. Because she did not want to be exploited again, and she was sleeping in an isolated place with her child, she became depressed and decided to commit suicide. She did not want her child to have such a life. She went to a railway track with her child in her arms and lay waiting for the train to crush them. As she was laying there, she heard an old man crying in anguish and she found out the man was a cripple and an invalid, and could not do anything by himself. He needed food and water. So, she went and begged to get him food and water.

She felt that the old man was the voice of God reminding her of her promise. She called him Krishna. She said God was reminding her that she had a higher purpose in life than to commit suicide. She had something to contribute to this life. Later, she was sitting under a tree wondering, I have nothing, I have no-one, how can I help others? Then she saw a branch of the tree that a woodman had cut violently, and the branch was hanging by a single string. That branch was giving her and her child shade. So, she thought, this is the answer. Even though I have been beaten down like this tree, still I can be useful to others.

She started to look for homeless, abandoned, orphaned children, and she became their mother, taking care of them. She would beg and sing songs so that people felt moved and gave her food, water and medical supplies to take care of those in need. After some time, people saw that she was making a difference in others' lives. So, they build an orphanage for her. Over the years she took care of over 1000 children. She made a tremendous difference in their lives. Today, she is known as the mother of orphans.

Many of the children she took care of became lawyers, other became medical doctors, farmers, and so on. Her service was recognized and she was given many awards internationally, as well as receiving awards from governors and even from the president of India.

In one of her speeches, she said the most important thing, the most meaningful thing she ever did in her life, was not about helping all these children, but it was helping one person. One day an old man came to her orphanage seeking help: He was starving; he was sick; he was homeless; he needed shelter. After a few minutes she recognized him. He was her ex-husband, the same one who tried to murder her years before. When she saw him, she wept, but she said to him, "When you left me to die, I was homeless in rags, now you are homeless in rags and I have a nice place with so many people." She said the most meaningful thing in her life was not helping the orphans, but forgiving him. She said, "I will give you shelter, but not as your wife but as your mother."

When people visited the orphanage, she would introduce her ex-husband: "This is my eldest son and sometimes he is very naughty." As she told the story, she introduced to the audience a young girl who was smiling joyfully. She said: "She was the one who was born under the cow, and she is now a medical doctor and is taking care of one of the orphanages."

Sindhutai said, "I consider all the tragedies in my life to have been gifts to empower me so I can make a difference in other people's lives." She considered this as God comforting her: "My life has been a road with many thorns, but I made friends with those thorns and my life became beautiful and I can share the beauty with many."

This is one example of properly grieving when we are in pain. When we get hurt and we are in pain, life will always tell us, flip the coin and you will see a blessing. Unfortunately, sometimes we get so consumed with our own pain, so we do not see the other side of the coin. We get stuck in revenge, anger and resentment. It becomes a poison for our spirit.

A. What life lesson did you learn from the story of Sindhutai?

B. Have you ever been hurt by someone or a group of people to the point you can't forgive? If yes explain!!! Have you ever hurt someone who needed your apology? If yes explain.

C. Make a commitment to forgive today

D. Make a commitment to apologize today

1. Now identify the person who hurt you and the person you have hurt

2. Call that person

3. If she/he does not respond leave a message

4. Say this, "Hello, I'm calling to let you know that I was very hurt by what happened between us and I choose to forgive. I am not holding anything against you."

Or "I am calling you to ask for your forgiveness. I am sorry for what happened. What can I do to make things better?"

5. If the person is not around, send an e-mail, send an SMS, or write a letter

6. Listen to the person's response and say thank you without going into too much reasoning or justification.

7. If the person died, write a letter, read it out loud and burn it

8. Do it today, tomorrow may be too late to free yourself.

V. The Principle of Choice

According to the *Merriam-Webster Dictionary*, choosing is an act of selecting or deciding when faced with two or more possibilities. It is also a careful selection, a preference, the right or ability to make, or possibility of making, such a selection. It is having a range of possibilities from which one or more may be selected. Let us look into the principle of choice.

1. Principle of choice

The principle of choice is rooted in the ability to make decisions without fear. We all have this ability, but it goes together with responsibility. It is the ability to respond properly regardless of our internal struggles, our pain and fears. We were created free and no one should be the owner of our lives except ourselves. All your decisions after you become conscious of your existence are your decisions. In fact, there are no wrong choices. There are immature choices and we learn from those choices and grow; or we do not learn, and we keep repeating them again and again until we learn the lesson life is trying to teach us. Einstein said, "Insanity is doing the same thing over and over again and expecting different results."

If fact, you become the result of your constant choices. Your everyday choices make you who you are. You want to know someone's destiny? Observe they daily choices. If they drink coffee with a lot of sugar and milk every day then you know that they have a high probability to get diabetes in the coming years. Someone who eats a lot of meat and high-fat foods every day and does not exercise will certainly gain weight and be exposed to a possible heart attack. Our daily choices create the kind of life we have.

Besides birth and death, we always have choices. We do not choose to be born; it is someone else's choice for us, ultimately our parents. We do not choose to die unless it is by suicide, and even then, sometimes people fail to commit suicide.

Some choices help us grow and mature, and others can lead us to unnecessary suffering. Choices based on fear, anger, jealousy, envy, revenge or greed will lead to unnecessary suffering. The root of unnecessary suffering is our incapacity to process pain. As the good book says "There is no fear in love" (1 John 4:18). Therefore, fear is the absence of love. Choices based on love, patience, understanding and courage lead to maturity and peace.

Fear is part of our everyday lives: We afraid of people, dangerous animals, afraid of the future, afraid of being sick, afraid of suffering, pain, and afraid of death. At the root of all fear is the fear of death. This is also known as existential anxiety!!! If you can identify your biggest fear, you will see it is that fear which is unconsciously driving your life. All your decisions, conscious or unconscious, small or big, are coming from that fear.

Fear of everything can also make us paranoid or phobic, and can affect our health. This kind of fear mostly comes from our past painful experiences, strange imagination and uncertainty of the future. Another fear we all have unconsciously or consciously is the fear of not being loved by others, or being ostracized or excommunicated from a group. This kind of fear can destroy our inner power, the ability to function normally.

2. The issue of destiny

Destiny is a complex philosophical issue that every tradition deals with. From a personal development perspective there are certain things we do not choose, such as the date we are born, the place we are born, or the time in history. Possibly parents do their part, but there is a factor that can be considered destiny. We do not have any choice. Additionally, during our lifetime, we make a lot of mistakes. However, there is a force above us that keeps influencing us in order to achieve what we are destined for in this life. This force does not actually force us, but rather influences us to make the right choices or to learn from the bad choices we make.

As we grow in wisdom, we realize that some choices help us grow in maturity and others lead to unnecessary suffering. Choices based on fear, anger, jealousy, envy, revenge or greed will cause unnecessary suffering and choices based on the principles of transformation, truth, love and restoration will lead to maturity, success and development.

3. The power within

Jewish psychiatrist Victor Frankl said: "Between stimulus and response there is a gap. In this space is our power to choose our response. In our response lies our growth and our freedom." Frankl discovered the principle of choice when he was tortured in Nazi concentration camps during the Holocaust in World War II. He observed people reacting to torture and extreme pain. He realized that some people, when going through pain, would cry, scream and curse. They would be out of control when they were tortured by the Nazis. He also observed others who would remain calm and silent as they went through the same kind of torture. He thought to himself that he would like to understand the underlying reason why people reacted so differently.

As he went through the experience himself, he discovered the truth about human responsibility to make choices no matter what the circumstances of our lives might be. What helped him survive, he said, was the fact that he dreamed and hoped that he could teach this principle to his future students. Victor Frankl discovered his inner power to make choices no matter the circumstances he was facing.

Although Frankl emphasized free will, to this we must add two other factors that make us who we are. We are also influenced by society, the environment we grow up in, and the kind of people who educated us since birth. Additionally, we are also born with some natural tendency to be an outgoing extrovert or more of a reflective introvert, as well as some specific genetic and biological traits.

No matter the environment you were born in, no matter the natural tendencies you have, no matter your biological make up, you still have free will and you must tap into your inner power in making decisions on crucial matters. Fear can prevent you from making free and responsible choices at critical times in your lives. Most people are not in touch with their inner power. They give power to the outer authorities, such as those in positions of power. This is not about disrespect to leaders, but external authorities can abuse power if they are not themselves in tune with their own inner power. They might want to control the lives of others by refusing to give them freedom of choice. On the other hand, fear of external authority keeps you away from freedom of choice, from exercising your free will, the power within you. The fear of outer authority can enslave you and make you emotionally and spiritually dependent on people.

Fear of outer authority can be a problem for personal growth. For example, one might wonder why, in the story of Adam and Eve in Genesis, God allowed Adam and Eve to make their own choices in the garden of Eden. God allowed them to make their choices freely even though he had forbidden them to eat of the fruit of the tree of the knowledge of good and evil. Well, we disobeyed God, but we also learned about the pain of separation and the importance of returning to God. We have dealt with the consequences of our choices. That is why, when you coach others or advise them, do not make decisions for people. Teach them the possible consequences and let them make their own choices. Be honest if you don't agree with their choices, but respect their choices. Then, if they fail, they won't blame you and they will learn from it. Mature people learn from their failures and continue to grow. Only stupid people do not learn from their mistakes and therefore cannot walk the path of wisdom.

In reality, no one should deprive you of your freedom of choice. If someone is doing it, then that means you have given them the power to do it. Parents sometimes think they should make all the decisions for their children. Unfortunately, this can destroy their inner ability to make choices when they become adults. Even at a young age, you can suggest possibilities to the child and let them decide. This approach educates their inner power. If we don't do that, we destroy their ability to make free choices in critical times. Some people are so undecided so that they always expect someone else's approval before they make a decision. Parents must help their children make free choices in order to strengthen their inner power and sharpen their intuition. This kind of education is also a foundation for responsible leadership.

Power and authority

There is a difference between authority and power: Authority is given to us to exercise power. Power is the ability to lead, guide and influence others. Authority is external and power is internal. Authority is form and power is essence. For example, the Bible, the Qur'an and the Torah, which we call sacred texts or scriptures, are supposed to guide us in the right direction. However, when sacred scripture replaces intuition, the inner self, we begin to seek power outside of ourselves. Sometimes we use verses to judge, kill, hate, exclude, fight, and divide, and then we justify it through the same scripture.

We use an external symbol to exercise power. Social positions, symbols, rituals and titles are guides and not inner power. Unfortunately, these things are used to control others to do what we want, or what we think is right. Either we force others to do our will or we use violence. Therefore, we can see terrorists using the same Qur'an to justify their acts of violence. We also see in history the use of the Bible to support the Crusades. The Bible has been used to support colonialism, imperialism, slavery, etc.

Some leaders believe their power is outside of themselves, so when they feel threatened, they become extremists and they start using their external symbols, such as texts, titles, money and so forth, to fight others. Our choices should come from our inner power and not from outside influence. You can have authority without power just as you can have power without authority. A good leader must integrate internal power (essence) and external authority (form).

4. Intuitive fear

Gavin de Becker, author of *The Gift of Fear*, explained that intuitive fear is different from other types of fear. It is the fear we have in the presence of danger. In a dangerous situation, your intuition gives you a message that helps you make the right choice. This kind of fear is not about experience of the past, or anxiety or worry about the future, but a situation in the environment that tells you to protect yourself from danger. The body may react with sensations, an inner voice may speak, and emotion may give a sign.

There is a difference between general fear and intuitive fear. The fear coming from intuition is information that our inner power gives us. This fear is something that we experience in the present moment that gives us a signal that something is happening or is going to happen soon, depending on what we are hearing, seeing or feeling. Sometimes we meet someone for the first time and something unusual happens in us and we do not know why; but this experience is so real.

Intuitive fear is knowing something without knowing logically why. We are designed to protect ourselves from danger; it is part of our biological and spiritual makeup. The experience is first spiritual (intuition), then it influences the mind (perception), emotions (feelings) and the body (sensations). It is the expression of inner power.

5. Dreams

Dreams are not always messages from the spiritual world. According to Sigmund Freud, dreams are the manifestation of desires repressed in the subconscious. At night when we sleep, these repressed desires come back and manifest as a dream. For example, you may like a girl in your school or neighborhood, and want to marry her but there is no way for you to tell her due to some kind societal restrictions. If you strongly desire her you may one night dream that you are getting married to her. This dream is not counted as a spiritual message; rather it is known as the manifestation of your repressed desires. Understanding that this is your own desire will help you be more realistic in interpreting your dream. Some people believe so much in their dreams that they can make mistakes believing that the dream will come true. It usually won't.

We also experience nightmares, which are very often caused by stress, anxiety, trauma, depression or serious illness. Your body going through hardship can express itself through dreams. In Africa we tend to blame witches for nightmares. This is not to deny witchcraft but it is not always true to interpret your nightmare as witchcraft. You might see an angry old man from your village chasing you with a knife. You could even recognize his face, but it doesn't necessarily mean that this man is trying to harm you in real life. It could be due to your current state of stress or health, or a negative experience you had with that person.

Finally, many people do have dreams that are spiritual messages or prophecies of things to come. In general, major events such as a birth, special mission, meeting your spouse, facing your own mortality, or the death of a loved one, are in most cases communicated to you if you listen to your intuition and pay attention to your dreams. Nothing significant in our lives happens by chance. There are always signs and messages to inform us, but many of us close our spiritual antenna and we do not pay attention to the message from the universe.

6. Spiritual dimension

Spirituality answers questions like: Why do I exist? What is the meaning of my existence? What happens after death? There is already a seed planted in you since your birth: It is your divine calling. This is the purpose of your existence on earth. You will live only once. You must uncover it to live your life fully.

If you were given enough money to live a decent life and have no worry about your finances, what would you be focusing on? Your heart knows, and because you don't know exactly when you're going to die, stop postponing what you need to do today to live the life you were born for. You don't know if you will be alive tomorrow. Make the right choice today and live according to your destiny. Does your vision go beyond your physical reality? Will your vision keep you alive after you leave this world? Will people remember you 100 or 1000 years after you passed? Will you add something good to the collective consciousness of your generation and generations to come?

If you have trouble making a choice at a critical time in your life, make a sincere prayer, or a silent meditation, or a deep personal reflection. These practices will help you be in touch with your inner power, which is connected to the ultimate reality or God. Remember fear will always be a player. Therefore, live your life not your fear. It is also important to gather the correct information before jumping into anything. It's okay to ask other people's opinions, and get advice, but ultimately the choice is yours.

When you are taking your last breath, will you say I have lived my life fully without regret or will you say I wish I had lived my life as I feel called to? The answer is yours. Do not wait until you are on your deathbed; it will be too late.

Do not waste your time trying to do everything at the same time. Sometimes we are so disconnected from ourselves that we run everywhere and try to do everything. This is also a waste of time. If you're a doctor on a battlefield you're not going to waste your time trying to save those who will die anyway. You are going to focus on those who are wounded and have a chance to heal. This is similar to your life mission.

There are many great projects out there, so many businesses you can launch or join, so many organizations you like. However, it recommended to focus on something where you will make a difference. If your intervention or involvement is not necessary for the success of a project do not waste your time there. If the business is already flourishing, your presence won't be necessary. It is like those who are doing fine in the battlefield. They do not need medical treatment. If the project will die despite your intervention or involvement do not waste your time there either. It is like those who are so wounded that you know there is no hope for them. Why waste your time on a project or business that is dying anyway? It is a waste of your time.

If your intervention will make a significant contribution to the success of the project, the business or the organization, then commit yourself fully. Your talents and skills will be appreciated and valued where they are needed the most, not everywhere. This represents those who are wounded and still have a chance to heal and need a doctor's intervention.

I would like to conclude the principle of choice with this message from Pope Francis:

> There is the voice of God, which speaks kindly to the conscience, and there is the tempting voice which leads to evil ... One can learn to discern these two voices: they speak two different languages, that is to say that they have opposite ways of

knocking on the door of our hearts… The voice of God never forces us: God proposes himself; He does not impose himself. Instead, the evil voice seduces, assaults, forces: it evokes dazzling illusions, tempting but fleeting emotions. At first, she flatters us, she makes us believe that we are all-powerful, but then she leaves us empty inside and accuses us: "You are worth nothing." The voice of God, on the contrary, corrects us, with great patience, but always encourages us, consoles us: it always nourishes hope. The voice of God is a voice that has a horizon, while the voice of evil leads you to a wall, it pulls you back into a corner… The voice of the enemy distracts us from the present and wants us to focus on fears of the future or the sadness and mistakes of the past - the enemy does not want the present - it brings out bitterness, memories of wrongs suffered, of those who hurt us, … a lot of bad memories. On the other hand, the voice of God speaks in the present: "Now you can do good, now you can exercise the creativity of love, now you can give up the regrets and remorse that hold your heart in captivity." It inspires us, it moves us forward, but it speaks in the present: now.

7. Stories of choices based on intuition

Here are some stories that will help you distinguish between intuition and general fear.

Story 1: Fear of others

One night, I was coming home from work and jumped on the train very tired, seeking to get home and rest. I did not pay attention to where I was about to sit. I abruptly sat down near a white lady. She immediately jumped out of her seat and quickly moved away. There was a young couple and an older man on the train, all black people. They all saw the scene and were surprised too. They were wondering what was going on. I was embarrassed and shocked, thinking that I unintentionally did something stupid. At the next stop she quickly exited the train.

As I reflected, this lady was scared of something, but it was not me per se. I was not trying to hurt her. I didn't even speak to her. I had no gun; I was not drunk; the way I was dressed was not scary. I had never seen her before, but she was certainly afraid of what I reminded her of from her past. So, the only thing that can make sense is that she might have had a previous bad experience with someone like me. That is the only logical explanation I came up with. The other fact is we were all black on the train except her. She probably thought we would attack her because she was white. That is not intuitive fear.

Story 2: Trusting a stranger

This is a true story from the book *The Gift of Fear* by Gavin de Becker: A young lady was coming home from shopping and about to enter her apartment when she realized her entrance door was locked. She thought the neighbor locked it again. She got her keys out to open the door and some apples fell from her grocery bags. She heard a voice telling her, "I got it for you." It was a man's voice and she immediately did not like that voice. Her inner self, her inner authority, told her that something is wrong here, do not trust this voice. The guy came and told her, "I will help you get to your room with your stuff," and she responded "No." The guy tried to be nice and insisted, and she compromised. When the guy was about to enter her room, she tried to stop him and said she could do it herself. The guy joked about it and said to her, "I promise I will leave right after putting your stuff inside." She let him enter her apartment.

As soon as the guy entered the apartment, he pulled out a gun and pointed it at her head, and raped her for three hours. When he finished, he was going to kill her. He told her not to move, he was going to the kitchen to get a drink, and he would harm her if she moved. She responded in tears, "I will not move." On his way to the kitchen, he turned the volume up on the radio. She suddenly knew he was going to kill her, but did not want to use the gun. As he entered the kitchen, she stood up and silently walked slowly to open her door.

Outside, she locked the door and ran into the neighbor's house and they called the police.

What gave her the strength to do this was her inner authority. She finally listened to her inner voice, her intuition, which she had denied a few hours before. When she was telling the story, she was asked why she did not listen to her intuition in the first place? Her answer was, "I am not sure why. I just denied it." Why do we ignore our inner authority? It is because society does not encourage us to listen to and trust our intuition.

It is not always true that we can anticipate everything exactly 100%. There are things we cannot anticipate. However, when we pay attention to our inner power, we can see signs that can help us make the right decision at the right time. They are so many stories of when people denied their intuition and paid a huge price for it. There are also cases where some have listened to signs and made the best choices of their life. The most important is how you learned from the bad choices. Unless you learn from your bad choices you will repeat them. So, do not be afraid of making the wrong choice; be afraid of not learning the lesson. In that sense your mistakes can even be a blessing, an opportunity for growth.

Story 3: Seeing my mother for the last time

In December 2013, I felt a strong desire (intuition of the moment) to go and see my mother whom I had not seen for over 5 years. When I shared the idea with my wife, she was very unhappy about it. She felt like it would be a waste of money. Also, she felt that it would be hard for her during the holidays season as she would feel alone. She was pregnant with our second daughter, which could make things very difficult for the family without me. I listened to her concerns and I wanted to change my mind, but my heart was telling me to go see my mom. I struggled making that decision but finally I decided to go. This was the first time I spent a holiday far from my wife and kids.

I saw my mom on the night of January 2nd, 2014. We spoke in her room from 10pm to almost 3am. She shared a lot of stories and blessed me. She also told me that recently she had dreams about my father who built a house for her and was asking her to move there. My father had died almost 20 years before. After spending a few days with her I came back to New York. We communicated once a week in January and February, and on March 3rd she died. I was shocked because she got sick for a very short period. I reflected on it and realized that I made the right choice. I listened to my intuition so that I could see my mother for the last time before she passed into the other world.

We are all spiritual beings before being social beings. The experience of the presence of the spirit is undeniable when we are aligned with the present moment. What is being communicated to us is always a sign, so we should not ignore it. In fact, if we listen to our intuition, nothing will surprise us.

Scripture, tradition and rituals are outer authority and we value and respect them. But we should not replace our inner power with them. People in position are our outer authorities and we respect and love them, but they should not replace our inner authority. Your choices should not be based on your past experiences, your thoughts, and your negative emotions but on your inner power, your intuition. If someone says something to you and it resonates with you, your inner authority might be giving you a message. If not, respect that person and make your choice. If you realize you have made a wrong choice, learn from it and become wise.

Story 4: Trick to cash a stolen check

Life was hard. I had no job and no money due to the economic recession in the U.S. in 2008. One morning I decided to go to look for a job in downtown Atlanta, Georgia. While I was waiting in the parking lot, a white gentleman walked towards me. He said, "Would you like to work with us? We can pay daily." I asked him what kind of job. He replied, "Cleaning houses." I agreed and a few minutes later, his friend picked up us in his truck. We eventually got to the house and worked for about 6 hours. When we finished, I expected my money.

The guy asked me if it was okay to cash a check. I told him yes, thinking he was planning to give me my payment. We got into the pick-up truck again and drove to the bank. He gave me a check, with my name written on it. The check was for $4,000, and he told me to go in and cash it. I hesitated, and he said this was the only way he could pay me and buy some supplies. He also said that he could not cash it because his ID was expired. My intuition spoke at that time and said, do not trust this. But I was so eager to get my money that I accepted the deal.

Even when I was walking into the bank, I was still torn inside feeling that it was not the right choice to make. Still, I ignored it and walked up to the cashier. She took the check and asked me who gave it to me. I said my boss did. She then called the owner of the check to verify it. The owner told her that I had stolen the check from him. As I was waiting, the police came and arrested me.

Those guys set me up. They orchestrated the whole thing and I was being used by them to get what they wanted. I paid a huge price for this. I was in jail for few weeks and at the end of the trial the case was dropped. However, I suffered through it psychologically for several years. I learned the lesson: Listen to your inner voice in critical moments.

1. What influences your choices?
2. Who influences your choices?
3. Have you made mistakes that you keep regretting today?

4. What have you learned from your past mistakes? Is that helping you make better choices today?

General Conclusion

The five principles of personal development can be summed up as follows: Transformation involves discomfort, pain and the feeling of giving up. These feelings are positive signs that announce change, transformation or success. In everything, energy turns into matter over a period of time. This includes our efforts and actions as well as the mysterious aspect of the exact time when energy is transformed into matter.

The principle of truth teaches us that truth is universal. Each of us perceives it according to our current reality, so knowing how to listen to others is the healthiest activity to get closer to the truth.

The principle of love is to sacrifice yourself, to give of yourself, and invest unconditionally to grow in love. Don't make a life decision based on romantic love; it's not a lasting feeling.

The principle of restoration is to heal your emotional wounds and learn to rebuild broken relationships. Learn to control your emotions by controlling your negative thoughts.

The principle of choice: Listen to your intuition, it is the voice of God within you. Free yourself from your biggest fear. This is the way to live your life fully.

Make these five principles a habit. Whenever you face a personal or professional challenge, think about what principle of personal development needs to be applied in that context. Then try to apply it and see the results for yourself. Success in personal development is not based only on intellectual knowledge of the principles alone but mostly on their application. There is a science behind success. In reality nothing happens by chance. You can apply these principles in all dimensions of your life (individual, family, community, nation, and in the context of international relations).

The principle remains the same, and it is up to you to adapt it according to your needs. If you are entrepreneurs, managers, organization or opinion leaders, applying the principles of personal development is the best chance for success. However, remember the main thing, success is balancing your life so you don't die with regrets.

Here is an example of a wealthy politician from New York who worked very hard to become mayor of his city. Sadly, he neglected his wife and daughter while trying to reach his 20-year goal. He made his dream come true by becoming mayor and he was very proud of himself. However, his wife and daughter were left out of the process. He was an absent husband and father.

During his successful political life, he did not anticipate the worst-case scenario. He visited his daughter and told her the bad news: He had cancer that was growing very quickly in his body. He only had three months to live. On his deathbed, reflecting on his life, he realized that his money, the titles and positions he had fought for all his life no longer meant much to him. He asked to see his daughter so that he could share with her his regret at not being present for her. When she received her father's request, she refused to come and see him. She replied, "I don't want to pretend; I don't think I have a father. I can't go to meet you." When the mayor received the message, he became sad and cried. His daughter knew he was her biological father but not her relationship father due to his unbalanced lifestyle. Now, it was certainly too late to rebuild 20 years of father-daughter relationship.

The lesson is not to sacrifice your family for your job, your career, or some mission. It could lead to the loss of your meaningful relationships and to having regrets on your deathbed. As the Bible says, "What will it profit a man to gain the whole world and lose his soul? Or what will a man give in exchange for his soul?" (Mark 8:36) Would you like your family to be around you on the day you take your last breath? There is no better feeling than this. So, love your family.

I will conclude with a quote from Mahatma Gandhi:

> God, help me to tell the truth to the strong and to avoid telling lies to the weak. If you give me success, do not take away my humility. If you give me humility, do not take away my dignity. God, help me to see the other side of the medal. Don't let me blame others of treason just because they don't think they like me. God, teach me to love people as

I love myself and to judge me as I judge others. Please, don't let me be proud if I succeed, or fall in despair if I fail. Remind me that failure is the experience that precedes triumph. Teach me that forgiving is the most important in the strong and that revenge is the most primitive sign in the weak. If you take away my success, let me keep my strength to succeed from failure. If I fail people, give me courage to apologize and if people fail me, give me courage to forgive them. God, if I forget you, please do not forget me.

Peace!

End ~

Bibliography

Allport, Gordon W. *Becoming: Basic Considerations for a Psychology of Personality*. Yale University Press, 1983.

Brooks, David. *The Road to Character*. Random House Trade Paperbacks, 2016.

Brown, Steven Ravett. *Structural Phenomenology: An Empirically Based Model of Consciousness*. Peter Lang, Inc., 2005.

Carnegie, Dale. *How to Win Friends and Influence People*. Simon & Schuster, 2009.

Cialdini, Robert B. *Influence: The Psychology of Persuasion*. Harper Business, 2006.

Covey, Stephen R. *Principle-Centered Leadership*. Free Press, 1991.

Covey, Stephen R. *The 7 Habits of Highly Effective People*. Simon & Schuster, 2004.

de Becker, Gavin. *The Gift of Fear*. Little, Brown and Company, 1997.

Devine, Tony, Joon Ho Seuk, and Andrew Wilson. *Cultivating Heart and Character: Educating for Life's Most essential Goals*. Character Development Publishing, 2000.

Duhig, Charles. *The Power of Habit: Why We Do What We Do in Life and Business*. Random House, 2014.

Frager, Robert, and James Fadiman. *Personality and Personal Growth*. Pearson, 2012.

Fromm, Erich. *The Art of Loving*. Continuum, 2020.

Fuhrman, Joel. *Eat to live: The Amazing Nutrient-Rich Program for Fast and Sustained Weight Loss*. Little, Brown and Company, 2011.

Heifetz, Ronald A. *Leadership Without Easy Answers*. Harvard University Press, 1998.

Heifetz, Ronald A., Marty Linsky, and Alexander Grashow. *The Practice of Adaptive Leadership*. Harvard Business Press. 2009.

Hill, Napoleon. *Think and Grow Rich*. The Napoleon Hill Foundation, 2017.

Hill, Napoleon. *Outwitting the Devil: The Secrets to Freedom and Success*. The Napoleon Hill Foundation, 2020.

Keagan, Robert, and Lisa Laskow Lahey. *Immunity to Change: How to Overcome It and Unlock the Potential in Yourself and Your Organization*. Harvard Business School Publishing Corporation, 2009.

Leaf, Caroline. *Who Switched off my Brain? Controlling Toxic Thoughts and Emotions*. Wesscott Marketing, 2008.

Maxwell, John C. *Developing the Leader Within You*. Thomas Nelson, 2005.

Maxwell, John C. *How Successful People Lead: Taking Your Influence to the Next Level*. Center Street, 2013.

McIntosh, Gary L., and Samuel D. Rima, Sr. *Overcoming the Dark Side of Leadership: The Paradox of Personal Dysfunction*. Baker Books, 1998.

Messick, Mark L. *The Art of Success: How to Crush Failure and Reach for the Stars*. Grizzly Publishing, 2015.

Pavlina, Steve. *Personal Development for Smart People: The Conscious Pursuit of Personal Growth*. Hay House, 2008.

Peale, Norman Vincent. *The Power of Positive Thinking*. Touchstone, 2003.

Robbins, Tony. *Awaken the Giant Within: How to Take Immediate Control of Your Mental, Emotional, Physical and Financial Destiny!* Simon & Schuster, 1992.

Rohr, Richard. *Adam's Return*. The Crossroad Publishing Company, 2004.

Rohr, Richard. *The Naked Now: Learning to See as the Mystics See*. The Crossroad Publishing Company, 2009.

Ruiz, Don Miguel. *The Four Agreements: A Practical Guide to Personal Wisdom*. Amber-Allen Publishing, 2018.

Schwartz, J. David. *The Magic of Thinking Big*. Fireside, 1987.

The Arbinger Institute. *Leadership and Self Deception: Getting out of the Box*. Berrett-Koehler Publishers, 2002.

Tipping, Colin. *Radical Forgiveness: A Revolutionary Five-Stage Process to Heal Relationships, Let Go of Anger and Blame, and Find Peace in Any Situation*. Sounds True, Inc., 2009.

Tolle, Eckhart. *The Power of Now: A Guide to Spiritual Enlightenment*. New World Library, 2010.

Wattles, Wallace D. *The Science of Getting Rich*. Merchant Books, 2019.

Whitelaw, Ginny, and Betsy Wetzig. *Move to Greatness: Focusing the Four Essential Energies of a Whole and Balanced Leader*. Nicholas Brealey Publishing, 2008.

Exam Preparation: A Guide for Your Certificate in Personal Development

Instructions: There are 100 questions in total and each correct answer equals 1 point.

You need 60 points to pass the exam and receive your certificate.

1. According to Richard Rohr, how many steps are needed for a transformation of self? (Select the correct answer)

   A. 6 steps
   B. 5 steps
   C. 4 steps
   D. 3 Steps

2. "Until you make the unconscious conscious, it will direct your life and you will call it fate." Who is the author of this quote?

   A. Karl Jaspers
   B. Carl Rogers
   C. Carl Jung
   D. Karl Marx

3. "One does not become enlightened by imagining figures of light, but by making the darkness conscious." Who is the author of this quote?

   A. Carl Jung
   B. George A. Sheehan
   C. Ken Wilber
   D. Carl Rogers

4. "Shadow Boxing" means

   A. Blaming others when you are hurt
   B. Playing the victim when things go badly
   C. Being self-reflective and introspective when things do not go well
   D. Attacking back whenever you feel hurt

5. Personal development is defined as the process of (Check the correct answer)

   A. Self-transformation
   B. Self-maturation
   C. Personal growth
   D. All the above

6. The 4 main dimensions of human being are ... (Which one is linked to the principle of choice?)

   A. Intellectual
   B. Emotional /socio-emotional
   C. Physical
   D. Spiritual

7. Personal development training helps people harmonize their being ...

   A. With their religion

   B. With their superiors

   C. With their life purpose

   D. With their friends

8. Passion means

   A. Falling in love

   B. Suffering

   C. Fear of the other

   D. Courage

9. Who is the author of this assertion? "Personal development is not psychotherapy but constant self-improvement of all areas of the human dimension."

   A. Danilo Martuccelli

   B. Franck Jaotombo

   C. Stephen R. Covey

   D. Max Weber

10. The theory of levels of consciousness was developed by

   A. Stephen R. Covey

   B. Ken Wilber

   C. Robert Kiyosaki

   D. Abraham Maslow

11. What is the highest level of consciousness according to Ken Wilber?

A. Ethnocentrism

B. Worldcentrism

C. Egocentrism

D. Cosmocentrism

12. In African initiation, there are three basic elements that help transition from adolescence to adulthood. They are:

A. Self-control

B. Keeping secrets

C. Respect for elders

D. Dominating others

13. "Education is the most powerful weapon that we can use to change the world." This quote is from

A. Martin Luther King Jr.

B. Patrice Lumumba

C. Nelson Mandela

D. Thomas Sankara

14. In 2018, a report of the African Development Bank stated that the unemployment rate of vulnerable jobs in Ivory Coast was

A. 50 to 60%

B. 40 to 80%

C. 70 to 90%

D. 60 to 70%

15. The main objective of personal development training is to help people (Check the incorrect answer)

    A. Improve public speaking
    B. Set clear and realistic goals
    C. Gain self-knowledge
    D. Always win a debate

16. One pioneer of modern-day personal development is

    A. Émile Durkheim
    B. Émile Coué
    C. Émile Zola
    D. Emile Hirsch

17. In 2006, a film on personal development by Bob Proctor and Jack Canfield, written by Rhonda Byrne, became part of popular consciousness. This film is titled

    A. The Revolution
    B. The Secret
    C. Power
    D. Almighty

18. Wallace D. Wattles, American author (1860 - 1911), wrote the classic book on personal development in 1910. What was the title of the book?

    A. The Power of Money
    B. The Law of Attraction
    C. The Science of Getting Rich
    D. The Power of Love

19. In 1937, Napoleon Hill (1883-1970) wrote one of the most famous personal development books. What was the title of the book?

    A. Think and Grow Rich
    B. Think Rich and Grow
    C. Grow and Be Rich
    D. Trust Yourself

20. The book "How to Win Friends and Influence People," published in 1936 was written by...

    A. Napoleon Hill
    B. Bob Proctor
    C. Dale Carnegie
    D. Norman Vincent Peale

21. Norman Vincent Peale's bestseller for over 10 years on The New York Times list, published in 1952, is titled

    A. The Power of Positive Thinking
    B. The Power to Defeat the Other
    C. The Power of Critical Thinking
    D. The Power of Forgiveness

22. Personality as an ego is a subjective identity, and subjective identity is socially constructed. Who developed this idea?

    A. Carl Rogers
    B. Abraham Maslow
    C. Carl Jung
    D. Karl Jaspers

23. The concept of the subjective self or "false self" was developed by

    A. Richard Rohr
    B. Thomas Merton
    C. Thomas Hobbes
    D. Thomas Jefferson

24. The word "Persona" is derived from the Latin word for

    A. Consciousness
    B. Ego
    C. Mask
    D. Aura

25. Ego in the specific context of Personal Development, is attachment to............................ as the main sources of our happiness. (Check the correct answer)

    A. An idea
    B. A title and position
    C. Material possessions
    D. All the above

26. The work of an economist in the 1980s amply demonstrated that poverty was not only a matter of income but also involved a wider range of deprivation in health, education, and standard of living. His name is...

   A. Amartya Sen
   B. John Maynard Keynes
   C. Adam Smith
   D. Joseph E. Stiglitz

27. "Poverty is not just a lack of money; it is not having the capability to realize one's full potential as a human being." This quote is from

   A. Karl Marx
   B. Amartya Sen
   C. Joseph Smith
   D. John Maynard Keynes

28. Who is the author of this famous quote? "Africa doesn't need strong men, it needs strong institutions."

   A. Nelson Mandela
   B. Kwame Nkrumah
   C. Barack Obama
   D. Muammar Al-Gaddafi

30. "We also know what it is like to be aware of something (when awake or dreaming) rather than not being aware of it. This everyday understanding of consciousness based on the presence or absence of experienced phenomena provides a simple place to start." The author of this quote is

    A. Steven R. Brown

    B. Ken Wilber

    C. Robert William

    D. Robert Gordon

31. Development of consciousness means ...

    A. Self-awareness

    B. Self-knowledge

    C. Self-mastery

    D. All the above

32. A symptom of narcissism is the inability to

    A. Accept criticism

    B. Love animals

    C. Tell great stories

    D. None of the above

33. "When you do not have external possessions you find them more important but when you do have them, you will know that they are not enough for inner satisfaction of life." Who is the author of this quote?

   A. Dietrich Eckart
   B. Eckart von Hirschhausen
   C. Eckhart Tolle
   D. Eckart Marsch

34. "Happiness is not directly linked to how much money you earn." The findings of this research were published by psychologists from

   A. Harvard University
   B. University of California
   C. Purdue University and University of Virginia
   D. University of Pennsylvania

35. If you want to know someone's destiny, observe …

   A. How he looks
   B. How he dresses
   C. His daily habits
   D. All the above

36. "Watch your thoughts, they become your words; watch your words, they become your actions; watch your actions, they become your habits; watch your habits, they become your character; watch your character, it becomes your destiny." The author of this quote is

   A. Lao Tzu
   B. Mao Zedong
   C. Mao Xiaotong
   D. Mao Tse-tung

37. "You cannot be present while thinking, your thoughts are taking you into the past or into the future." The author of this assertion is...

   A. Ken Wilber
   B. Eckhart Tolle
   C. René Descartes
   D. René Depestre

38. The word emotion comes from the Latin "Emotus." It means....

   A. Fear
   B. Disturbance
   C. Love
   D. Hate

39. In psychology, emotions are classified into two groups. The positive and the negative: Is "excitement" a negative or a positive emotion?

    A. Negative

    B. Positive

    C. Neither negative nor positive

    D. Both negative and positive

40. Negative emotions are the result of past:

    A. Negative thoughts

    B. Negative experiences

    C. Past bad decisions

    D. All the above

41. Managing negative emotions is key to success in

    A. Business

    B. Marriage

    C. School

    D. All the above

42. Most people would like to reason with it, but it escapes reason and resides only in spiritual experience. This assertion is referring to

    A. The ego

    B. Thought

    C. Emotion

    D. The inner self

43. To live is to continue to exist positively in the collective consciousness after death. Check the name that does not fit here.

    A. Jesus Christ
    B. Mahatma Gandhi
    C. Mother Teresa
    D. Adolf Hitler

44. The concept of God as an old white man sitting on his throne and looking down on us from above first spread in popular consciousness through which tradition?

    A. Jewish
    B. Christian
    C. Greco-Roman
    D. African

45. The death of the ego in the process and the emergence of cosmocentric consciousness is mostly possible in

    A. Dogmatic religions
    B. The practice of authentic spirituality
    C. Culture
    D. Traditions

46. The five universal principles of personal development are ... Which one deals with inclusive leadership?

    A. Transformation

    B. Love

    C. Choice

    D. Restoration

    E. Truth

47. Personal development theory suggests that growth occurs when our responses to life's challenges are ... (Check the incorrect answer)

    A. Self-reflective

    B. Introspective

    C. Defensive

    D. All the above

48. Personal development works when

    A. Culture is aligned with universal principles

    B. Culture is aligned with the values of the community

    C. Culture is aligned with Western world values

    D. Culture is aligned with personal ideas

49. What is a principle?

    A. A cultural law

    B. A universal law

    C. A societal law

    D. Community law

50. Culture comes from the Latin word "cult," which means (Check the incorrect answer)

    A. A way of seeing God
    B. Beliefs, rituals and traditions
    C. Universal principles
    D. Belief in a divinity

51. Our life choices should be based on

    A. Universal principles
    B. African culture if we are African
    C. Western culture if we are Westerners
    D. Asian culture if we are Asian

51. $E = mc^2$ is the fundamental theory that explains the principle of

    A. Truth
    B. Transformation
    C. Love
    D. Choice
    E. Restoration

52. The essence of the principle of transformation consists of

    A. Do not give up when you are challenged
    B. Give up when you are challenged
    C. Whenever you are discouraged, give up
    D. Whenever there is discomfort, give up

53. A successful life consists of connecting your passion to your

    A. Vocation
    B. Family tradition
    C. Best friend's passion
    D. Religious beliefs

54. There is a hidden talent in all of us, we can discover it by (Check the right answer)

    A. Prayer and meditation
    B. Listening to our heart
    C. Self-evaluation/assessment
    D. All the above

55. There are four types of leader, each of us is good at one of them. Which type of leader has the strengths needed for conflict resolution and diplomacy?

    A. Organizer
    B. Visionary
    C. Collaborator
    E. Driver

56. As a leader, to make a critical decision with your team members you must ... (Check the incorrect answer)

    A. Listen to everyone first
    B. Ask questions to understand different views
    C. Harmonize different team members' perspectives
    D. Make a uniliteral decision

57. The first step toward formulating a vision statement is to figure out ....

    A. What problem you want to solve
    B. How to make a lot money
    C. How to convince others about your product
    D. Ask questions about the market

58. The maximum number of words for a good mission statement should be between

    A. 30 to 35 words maximum
    B. 20 to 25 words maximum
    C. 35 to 45 words maximum
    D. 45 to 100 words

59. Between your dream and reality there is a gap, a void, and this void is filled with

    A. A clear understanding of your life purpose
    B. A better understanding of your job description
    C. A clear realistic plan
    D. Working hard everyday

60. The ability to effectively manage one's time consists of mastering one's weekly activities through the time management matrix. It was developed by

    A. Stephen R. Covey
    B. Abraham Maslow
    C. Ken Wilber
    D. Tony Robbins

61. In the time management matrix, the most important activity quadrant is ....

   A. Not urgent and important

   B. Urgent and important

   C. Not urgent and not important

   D. Urgent and not important

62. Personal development emphasizes

   A. Preventive health

   B. Curative treatment

   C. Indigenous medicine

   D. A mixed of curative and indigenous treatment

63. What is the first and most important need of an adult body for a healthy life? (Check the correct answer)

   A. Eat a lot of meat

   B. Drink 2.5 ounces of water a day

   C. Eat sugar-based food

   D. Drink a lot milk

64. Calories come from what we consume each day, and calories turn into fat in the body. So, to burn calories you need to ... (Check the correct answer)

   A. Drink cola after each meal

   B. Drink hot coffee after each meal

   C. Exercise regularly

   D. Have 8 hours of sleep every night

65. Habits that get you out of poverty are (Check the correct answer)

    A. Spending whatever you earn because life is short
    B. Getting into debt to buy what you don't really need
    C. Spending what you have because money comes and goes
    D. Saving money and investing

66. Personal development encourages leadership and entrepreneurship training in Africa in order to ....

    A. Reduce the unemployment rate
    B. Reduce poverty
    C. Improve the overall life of the African people
    D. All of the above

67. The principle of transformation is to ... (Check the correct answer)

    A. Make the impossible, possible
    B. Keep investing when it is hard
    C. Never give up in difficult times
    D. All the above

68. Everything that physically exists was first thought out mentally. This statement explains the principle of

    A. Choice
    B. Love
    C. Restoration
    D. Transformation

69. The story of the elephant and the six blind men explains ...
(Check the correct answer)

   A. The universality of truth

   B. The importance of humility

   C. Understanding personal truth

   D. All the above

70. When a wise man points at the moon, an idiot looks at his finger. This statement explains the principle of

   A. Love

   B. Transformation

   C. Truth

   D. Restoration

71. Individual or personal truth is discovered by (Check the correct answer)

   A. Introspection

   B. Blaming others

   C. Arguing with others

   D. Defensiveness

72. As one cannot see the other side of the moon, there is also a hidden side of the truth. This means (Check the correct answer)

   A. No one possess absolute truth

   B. Truth has a mysterious dimension

   C. We will never finish learning about the truth

   D. All the above

73. Our perception of the truth is influenced by (Check the correct answer)

A. Level of consciousness
B. Past experiences
C. Social conditioning
D. All the above

74. The famous quote "*Cogito, ergo sum*" meaning "I think, therefore I am" has put too much emphasis on one dimension of human beings (Check the correct answer)

A. Intuition
B. Intellect
C. Emotion
D. Will

75. The last step in scientific method to find the truth consists of ... Which one shows that scientific truth is contextual?

A. Hypothesis and research question(s)
B. Data collection and analysis
C. Recommendations
D. Limits of the study

76. Personal development is defined as "the conscious pursuit of personal growth by expanding self-awareness, self-knowledge and improvement of personal skills." Who is the author of this quote?

   A. Danilo Martuccelli
   B. Franck Jaotombo
   C. René Descartes
   D. Émile Coué

78. The emergence of developmental psychology goes back to the English psychologist William T. Preyer in 1882. He wrote a book entitled

   A. The Spirit of the Child
   B. The Heart of the Child
   C. The Mind of the Child
   D. The Emotion of the Child

79. A scientific fact is observable and verifiable; it is also referred to as (Check the correct answer)

   A. A universal truth
   B. An absolute truth
   C. A contextual truth
   D. A personal truth

80. The first step of active or empathic listening is to (Check the correct answer)

   A. Listen without interrupting
   B. Paraphrase what you hear
   C. Ask questions for clarification
   D. Observe body language

81. According to psychologist Erich Fromm, romantic love is a phenomenon one should not rely on when making lifetime decisions because ... (Check the correct answer)

   A. Love is not a mere feeling
   B. Romantic love is different from real love
   C. Romantic love does not last long
   D. All the above

82. Which one of these factors does not necessarily sustain real love?

   A. Beauty
   B. Sexuality
   C. Emotional transfer
   D. All the above

83. Emotional transfer is a phenomenon that is

   A. Always negative
   B. Always positive
   C. Either positive or negative
   D. Mostly negative

84. True love works because it is

    A. A cultural norm

    B. An emotional reaction

    D. A universal principle

    C. All the above

85. A relationship grows and remains healthy when love is manifested through (Check the correct answer)

    A. Independence

    B. Dependence

    C. Interdependence

    D. All the above

86. "If you want to make this world a better place, go home and love your family." This quote is from

    A. Teresa de Avila

    B. Sindhutai the mother of orphans

    C. Mother Teresa

    D. Oprah Winfrey

87. Whenever we are hurt, we react in different ways. Which one leads to personal growth

    A. Hurt back when you get hurt

    B. Withdraw and stop talking to the person who hurt you

    C. Heal yourself and others

    D. Keep resentment

88. We often hear people saying, "I have no choice" or "I had no other choice." This statement is untrue because we always have choices, but our choices are influenced by ....

    A. Fear
    B. Society
    C. Friends
    D. All the above

89. To make free choices without the influence of others and society we must listen to our...

    A. Intuition
    B. Authentic self
    C. Conscience
    D. All the above

90. What are the elements that influence our destiny?

    A. Social environment
    B. Our character
    C. Free will
    D. All the above

91. "Between the stimulus and the response, there is a space. In that space lies our power to choose our response. In our response lies our growth and our freedom." This is from...

    A. Ken Wilber
    B. Viktor Frankl
    C. Carl Jung
    D. Karl Jaspers

92. What is the difference between authority and power?

   A. Authority is internal, power is external

   B. Power is internal, authority is external

   C. Both are internal

   D. Both are external

93. There are different kinds of fear. Which one informs us of imminent danger?

   A. Fear of others

   B. Intuitive fear

   C. Fear of the past

   D. Fear of the future

94. Dreams represent a disguised fulfillment of a repressed wish. This assertion is from...

   A. Sigmund Freud

   B. Ken Wilber

   C. Carl Jung

   D. None of the above

95. Nightmares are very often caused by

   A. Stress

   B. Illness

   C. Trauma

   D. All the above

96. Dreams from the spirit world are also known as

    A. Prophetic messages
    B. Messages from the ancestors
    C. Messages from God
    D. All the above

97. The principle of choice is directly linked to the

    A. Physical dimension
    B. Emotional dimension
    C. Spiritual dimension
    D. Intellectual dimension

98. The principle of restoration is directly linked to the ...
    (Check the correct answer)

    A. Socio-emotional dimension
    B. Intellectual dimension
    C. Emotional dimension
    D. Physical dimension

99. To build a better and healthier society, we must focus on

    A. Punitive justice
    B. Restorative justice
    C. The death penalty
    D. All the above

100. "No one is born hating another person because of the color of their skin, their background or their religion. People must learn to hate, and if they can learn to hate, they can be taught to love, because love comes more naturally to the human heart than its opposite." This quote is from

A. Patrice Lumumba

B. Felix Houphouët-Boigny

C. Nelson Mandela

D. None of the above

GOOD LUCK :)

To contact Dr. Kone, email dkone@success4life.co

CPSIA information can be obtained
at www.ICGtesting.com
Printed in the USA
BVHW082249170521
607554BV00007B/1359